The
frazzled
factor

RELIEF FOR
WORKING MOMS

Karol Ladd
& Jane Jarrell

W PUBLISHING GROUP

www.wpublishinggroup.com

A Division of Thomas Nelson, Inc
www.ThomasNelson.com

The Frazzled Factor: Relief for Working Moms

Published by W Publishing Group, a Division of Thomas Nelson, Inc , PO Box 141000, Nashville, Tennessee 37214

W Publishing Group books may be purchased in bulk for educational, business, fundraising, or sales promotional use For information, please e-mail SpecialMarkets@ThomasNelson com

All Scripture quotations, unless otherwise indicated, are taken from the Holy Bible, New Living Translation, copyright © 1996 Used by permission of Tyndale House Publishers, Inc., Wheaton, Illinois 60189 All rights reserved

Other Scripture references are from the following sources.

The New American Standard Bible® (NASB), copyright 1960, 1962, 1963, 1968, 1971, 1972, 1973, 1975, 1977, 1995 by The Lockman Foundation Used by permission

The New Century Version® (NCV) Copyright© 1987, 1988, 1991 by Word Publishing, a Division of Thomas Nelson, Inc Used by permission All rights reserved

The NET Bible® (NET) Copyright© 2003 by Biblical Studies Press, L L C , www.NETBible com All rights reserved

The Holy Bible, New International Version (NIV) Copyright ©1973, 1978, 1984, International Bible Society Used by permission of Zondervan

The New King James Version® (NKJV), copyright 1979, 1980, 1982, Thomas Nelson, Inc , Publishers

The Amplified Bible (AMP), Old Testament copyright © 1965, 1987 by the Zondervan Corporation The Amplified New Testament copyright © 1958, 1987 by The Lockman Foundation Used by permission

Library of Congress Cataloging-in-Publication Data

Ladd, Karol
   The frazzled factor relief for working moms/by Karol Ladd and Jane Jarrell
     p cm
   ISBN 0-8499-4535-6
   1 Working mothers—Religious life 2 Child rearing—Religious aspects—Christianity 3 Work and family I Jarrell, Jane Cabaniss, 1961- II Title
   BV4529 18 L32 2004
   248 8'431—dc22

                                                                            2004017379

Printed in the United States of America

04 05 06 07 08 PHX 9 8 7 6 5 4 3 2 1

To our precious families:

Curt, Grace, and Joy
(Karol's family)

Mark and Sarah
(Jane's family)

Your love, support, and encouragement
are consistent blessings in our lives.

Contents

Contents

Acknowledgments

To all the working mothers we interviewed: thank you for sharing your trials and triumphs. May you find relief in the pages of this book.

To W Publishing Group and Debbie Wickwire: thank you for catching the vision and for partnering with us to make it happen. Your commitment to excellence will allow us to offer hope and encouragement to working mothers everywhere.

> Now to Him who is able to keep you from stumbling,
> and to make you stand in the presence of His glory
> blameless with great joy, to the only God our Savior,
> through Jesus Christ our Lord, be glory, majesty, dominion
> and authority, before all time and now and forever.
> JUDE 24–25 NASB

introduction

Enjoying the Ride
Encouragement for Frazzled Moms

*The secret of happiness is not in doing what
one likes but in liking what one has to do.*
— JAMES M. BARRIE

"Would somebody please stop the merry-go-round and let me get off?"

Do you remember feeling that way at the playground as a kid? The merry-go-round was nice when it was circling slowly, but when the bigger kids came and started spinning the ride faster and faster, all we wanted to do was get off!

Now as adults we feel similarly overwhelmed, only the merry-go-round is bigger. The "working mom merry-go-round" spins at a rapid pace with many life responsibilities: kids who need our love and attention, a dwelling place that demands our care and upkeep, and a job that requires our time and energy. Our hectic pace makes us feel out of control and frazzled. The problem is, we may not be able to stop the merry-go-round and get off like we did when we were kids on the playground.

Even if we were somehow able to slow down our frantic pace, our responsibilities often do not allow us to get off the working mom merry-go-round. So we must learn to adapt to the feel of the spin and put our faces to the breeze. We must learn ways not only to cope and survive as working moms, but to delight in the place God has set us. Our goal as working moms is not to hang on for dear life; rather, it is to ride with strength, wisdom, and discernment as we honor God in our circumstances and press forward in our lives with confidence.

The Frazzled Factor is here to help you have the best ride possible. We can't take away all of your responsibilities, but we can help you find peace in the process. In the chapters that follow, we want to help ease your anxiety, calm your stress, and regain your sense of control. Most important, we want to help you enjoy with pleasure the wonderful journey of being a mom.

Factoring Out the Frazzle

In this book, we have chosen to focus on seven areas that are important to working moms. We call them the top seven, because after polling numerous working moms, these were the areas they consistently mentioned. The top seven factors that tug at a working mother's heartstrings are guilt, parenting, relationships, business success, fun, personal refreshment, and spiritual growth. By factoring out the challenges in these areas, we hope to bring less frazzle and more victory to your life.

Frazzle is what happens to us when we feel as though an area of our life is out of control. It may come when we are stuck in rush-hour traffic trying to make it home before our daughter's dance recital. Frazzle may occur when a big project is due at work and you have a sick child at home. The state of being frazzled may occur every morning as you are rushing out the door with your month and discuss the chapters of this book together as a way of supporting each other. You can also use this book at your church for an evening class. Or you may want to join together with other readers at our web site: www.HighHeelsandHomeLife.com. At the web site you can join a chat room of other working moms and discuss thoughts spurred by our book or other issues.

Ultimately this book is meant to encourage you like a soothing friend and a thought-provoking mentor. It's based on the sure foundation of God's Word. Think of it as your pocket guide to possibilities and a better way of living the life of a working mom. Instead of being frazzled, you will become the queen of the merry-go-round!

The agony of enrolling your child in a
hyper-illness-sensitive day-care center.

Trust in the LORD and do good.
Then you will live safely in the land and prosper.
Take delight in the LORD,
and he will give you your heart's desires.
Commit everything you do to the LORD.
Trust him, and he will help you. . . .
The steps of the godly are directed by the LORD.
He delights in every detail of their lives.
PSALM 37:3–5, 23

chapter 1

The Guilt Factor

Finding Relief in the Midst of the Madness

> At work, you think of the children
> you've left at home. At home, you think
> of the work you've left unfinished.
>
> —Golda Meir

The intercom at the Dallas/FortWorth airport blared, "Flight 599, Flight 599, this is the final boarding announcement for Flight 599, departing for Orlando." Ella pushed her swollen feet back into her new black pumps, recently removed to help her make it through the new homeland security restraints. She grabbed her carry-on bag, minus the confiscated pointy tweezers, and hustled to make her flight.

She bumped and scooted her way through the warm, stale-smelling cabin to her cramped seat by the window. She put her carry-on bag in the overhead bin and settled herself. *Whew! I made it. Thank God, I made it.* There was not much Ella could do now, seeing as she was sequestered for the two-and-a-half-hour flight.

Sequestered. That sounded good: no e-mail, no phones, no laundry, and no guilt, right? Wrong. The ghost of guilt buckled up right next to her. In her feeble attempt to push the guilt aside, Ella mentally checked off her "keep-the-home-fires-burning" to-do list:

Meals prepared—check.

Laundry done—check.

Kissed husband and daughter good-bye—check.

Picked up clothes from the cleaners—check.

Planned kid transportation—check.

Now it was time to relax and enjoy the ride, right? Wrong again! Now it was time to focus on the presentation she was responsible for when the plane landed.

Ella was dealing with the difficulty of knowing that her seven-year-old daughter did not want her to leave—and neither did Ella. But she had no real choice. Ella was committed to an important opportunity, and she had to make the presentation. On the first evening of her business trip, Ella called home to say good night and could hear her daughter's tears begin to flow. "Mommy, please come home. I need you," Sarah pleaded.

This was tough. Fighting back her own tears, Ella promised to be home soon. After hanging up, she did what any respectable mother would do: she made a beeline for the vending machine down the hall. When the guilt begins taunting, sometimes chocolate softens the blow, but it won't soothe the inner struggle.

The Guilt Trip

Are you packed for the infamous guilt trip? Of course you are. As a working mom, you're no doubt loaded down with plenty of excess baggage for the journey. Guilt baggage comes standard with motherhood in a wide assortment of shades and sizes. Balancing work + marriage + financial needs + family + church +

extracurricular activities = guilt. Add your own variables to fit your personal equation. Ultimately life's demands take an over-whelming toll on us, leaving us exhausted, overwhelmed, and burdened with a load of guilt.

What is the toll that guilt takes on our lives? Author Harriet Lerner explains in her book *The Mother Dance*, "Guilt keeps mothers narrowly focused on the question, 'What's wrong with me?' and prevents us from becoming effective agents of personal and social change."[1] Needless to say, we could all fly a little higher if we weren't weighed down by the heaviness of guilt.

So what do we do about it? Let's take a brief trip down the road of understanding and relief to help us come to a practical place of peace in our hearts. We will examine three Ds along the way: *discover*, *determine*, and *decide*. We will discover the source of guilt, determine if the guilt is valid, and decide to respond instead of react. Ultimately, at the end of the road, each of us must be able to know in our hearts that we are in the place God wants us to be, for in that place we find peace and confidence.

In any battle, it is important to know who the enemy is and who it is not. The enemy is not our family, and the enemy is not our work. The enemy is the feeling of guilt, and it tends to play out through circumstances and people.

Discover the Source of Guilt

What presses your guilt button? Could it be when your child says, "Why do you always have to work late?" Or perhaps it's one of those questions from your boss, like, "Your kid is sick again?

> You may feel guilty about leaving your children for your work and guilty about leaving your work for your children. You will no doubt also feel guilty about being guilty.
>
> —Harriet Lerner

Wasn't he sick last week?" The guilt button may be pushed when your son says, "You never have time to help me with my homework." The tough reality is you know he's right, but there's little you can do about it when you're struggling just to finish your own workload.

Guilt can hit us from all sides. Even our pets can make us feel guilty for not giving them the attention they deserve! Guilt chips away at our consciences as we attempt to do the best we can at work and at home. With our natural bent to nurture others, women are especially gifted in the guilt game.

Whether our guilt is self-imposed or genuine, we must handle it in a healthy way. We can either demolish it or deal with it; but if we pretend it isn't there and stuff it deep down inside, our guilt will eventually erupt like a volcano, spewing out anger, resentment, and frustration at everyone in our path. Been there? Most of us have at one time or another. It's time to take our guilt and boldly face it head-on.

More than likely with your busy schedule, you have rarely taken time for introspection, and we're guessing that one of the last things you want to do is speculate about your own guilt. So we've made the following guilt self-check as simple and pain-free as possible. Don't belabor your responses; just take a few minutes to jot down the thoughts that immediately come to mind from the following questions.

What circumstances in my life tend to make me feel guilty?

_____

_____

_____

_____

If I'm going to be completely honest, the root of the guilt comes from _____ ,

_____

_____

I bring most of my guilt upon myself: Yes or No.

Certain people make me feel guilty: Yes or No.

If you circled "Yes," then jot down why these people make you feel guilty:

_____

After answering these questions, what can you say about your guilt? Does your guilt seem unfounded, or does it seem to be based on a solid problem or challenge? Did you identify certain people who make you feel guilty?

Take Rebecca, for instance. Her husband is the minister of a small church, and she works part-time as a nurse at the local hospital to help pay the bills. Several of the ladies in her husband's congregation make occasional stinging comments about how Rebecca never seems to be at home or that it's such a shame that her kids have to be in day care.

After several guilt-ridden years, Rebecca finally began to recognize that her guilt stemmed from the ladies' perceptions and assumptions. The truth is, Rebecca knew she was doing what was right for their family. She carried guilt that was heaped on her by other people.

Sometimes our guilt is not based on reality but rather on how people react to us. It is important to discover what makes us have those nagging feelings, because our first step toward fighting the enemy is recognizing it. As you answered the questions above, we hope you began to identify some of the sources of your guilt. Now let's determine what to do with it.

Determine If the Guilt Is Valid

Are your thoughts self-defeating, or are they self-assuring? Are you beating a dead horse or mounting a mighty stallion in your thought processes? What we allow to roll around in our brains can lead us in a positive direction, but if we are laden with guilt, we can become discouraged and defeated. So how do we hold on to reality and dump out the negative garbage?

As you discovered your own personal guilt hot spots in the self-examination above, you took the first step toward fighting the battle of guilt. Often the root of guilt comes down to the more telling question: should I be working outside the home as a mother? In other words, am I in the right place and doing what I should be doing? Take a moment right now to honestly write out the reasons you are working. It is important to get it out of your head and onto paper. Search your heart and be honest in your response.

_____

_____

_____

After writing out your reasons for working, answer the following questions:

Am I firm in my resolve that I am doing what I need to be doing? Yes or No.

When I think about coming before God with my reasons for working, I know I am doing what He wants me to be doing. Yes or No or Not Quite Sure.

Is there something I could be doing differently (working part-time or in another place or profession) that would give me more flexibility to juggle the responsibilities of home? Yes or No.

If you circled "Yes," write out several alternatives that come to mind.

_____

_____

_____

_____

In all truthfulness, sometimes our feelings of guilt may actually be our consciences bothering us because we are doing something we should not be doing. We should not dismiss guilt altogether in our lives, because sometimes guilt points us in the direction we ought to go. If God is using those tugging feelings to gently nudge us toward obedience, then we would be wise to heed His call. Often we heap those feelings onto our own pile of thoughts, and we may find ourselves buried in our own false assumptions and guilt. As you answered the questions above, it is our hope that they lead you to find the truth for your own life.

Delete Self-Imposed Guilt with PDA

A good guide for gutting out self-imposed guilt is encompassed in the acronym PDA. If you're up on technology, you know that a PDA is a personal digital assistant—a small, handheld computer that keeps track of schedules, addresses, phone numbers, and much more. For our purposes, however, PDA stands for "pray, determine, ask." Let's take a look at each of these components that help us get rid of self-imposed guilt.

Pray

When you are burdened by guilt in making a career decision or a choice for a child's future, it is essential to ask for God's direction. Many times Satan will use the guise of guilt to cloud our thinking and to reduce our effectiveness. But prayer is our powerful tool to conform our will to God's in His perfect timing. God knows our capabilities and He knows the future, so defer to His leadership first.

We can go confidently before the throne of grace and ask God for His direction. The Bible tells us to ask boldly and confidently for wisdom from God: "If you need wisdom—if you want to know what God wants you to do—ask him, and he will gladly tell you. He will not resent your asking" (James 1:5).

Determine

If God has called you to work outside the home, then don't waver. That's where you should be. Ultimately we must answer to God for our actions. If we are living outside of His will, then guilt tends to be a natural consequence. If we know we are in the place we are supposed to be or have no other choice but to work, then guilt can be an unnecessary distraction and cause us pain we were never meant to bear.

As you pray for discernment and use the self-assessment provided in this chapter, you will most likely come to a solid place of knowing you are in God's will. Now it's time to determine that you will not allow those feelings of false guilt to dominate your thought life. Determine to reject the false negatives and hold on to the real positives.

What are the positives we should hold on to? Here are a few on which to dwell:

- You can be confident you are in God's will.

- Difficulties help us (and our children) grow in strength and maturity.

- Your work is benefiting others (family income, the people at work, etc.).

- Your children are learning to be less self-centered and more God-centered.

- Your children are learning responsibility, independence, and a good work ethic.

Keep your eyes on the good things God can do through your work. Determine to dwell on these and dismiss the negative thoughts that creep in. The Bible tells us to keep our minds focused on what is true, noble, right, pure, lovely, admirable, excellent, and praiseworthy (see Philippians 4:8). Yes, there will be conflicts between work and family. Determine to work through these conflicts with God's wisdom, strength, and peace.

Ask

Seek wise counsel and encouragement from other working mothers who walk in your same high heels. We need affirmation from each other as we walk this rocky road of life. We need accountability to those of like mind in order to finish strong. Ask. It seems simple, but asking for advice or help from others can be difficult, especially when we want to appear as though we have it all together. We need to remember that we are not islands unto ourselves. We benefit from the help of others. The Bible says, "Two people can accomplish more than twice as much as one; they get a better return for their labor. If one person falls, the other can reach out and help. But people who are alone when they fall are in real trouble" (Ecclesiastes 4:9–10).

Recently we met an older woman who had retired from working full-time at a power company in Dallas. She mentioned that she felt it was her turn to give back to other businesswomen. Not only had she been a working mom, but her mother had also been a working mom. Now, as a grandmother, she felt it was time to use the wisdom and discernment God had given her to help other young working moms. She said she

> Of all the rights of women, the greatest is to be a mother.
> —Lin Yutang

simply wanted to be a mentor with a few solutions to busy schedules and, more important, a large dose of loving encouragement.

Don't hesitate to ask a friend to join you as you walk down this road. She may be your age or she may be older and may have already walked down the road before you. Either way, the journey of life is much smoother with a friend who understands.

Decide to Respond, Not React

"Late again," Lauren said in her smug, thirteen-year-old tone. Sandy felt her blood pressure rising as the backlash spewed from her mouth. "You try working two jobs with angry customers and a jerk for a boss! It's time you get off your little Princess Lauren throne and learn a little patience and respect!"

Oops! Often when our family members react negatively to our work/life conflict, we are tempted to lash out with an emotionally charged reaction instead of a healthy and healing response. When the emotional whining comes from our child or the blame flame is thrown from our teenager, let's choose to handle the guilt wisely. Falling apart or lashing out will only add more guilt to our load. We can reduce the stress level for ourselves and for our family if we pause to evaluate the situation and then offer a compromise or a reasonable explanation. Speak in love, because what our children really want to know is that we care. It can be healing and helpful to tell them that we share their frustration and sadness and that we want to be with them.

It is good for our children and husbands to learn through experience that life doesn't always turn out the way we want it to. We must do what we can to make the best of the situation and learn to accept the not-so-great parts of life. When your child is upset because there is a conflict between your work and something in his or her life, it is time to step back and evaluate. This becomes your chance to respond, not react.

First, consider whether your family member has a valid point. If you made an unwise decision, your child may be frustrated because he or she is paying the price by losing significant time with you. If that is the case, then you need to develop a workable compromise. For instance, if you are going to have to miss your daughter's recital because of a business trip, then ask someone to videotape the recital and schedule a time when you will sit down with your child, eat popcorn, and watch the show together.

Apologize when necessary, recognizing that you do make a bad decision now and then. Don't beat yourself up over the fact that you made an unwise move. You are human, just like everybody else. Help your family understand your mistake, ask for forgiveness when necessary, and move on. Your child will learn more about life when you apologize than if you try to act like you are perfect.

On the other hand, maybe your child is being unreasonable in expecting you to be there for all events at all times. You must evaluate if your child's demand is excessive. It is important for our children to learn that we cannot be there for them 24-7. We are not God, and it is not our job to hover over our children like helicopter moms. Our children learn and grow as a result of the tough bumps in life. If we are there to solve all of their problems, then when will they learn to make decisions on their own, ask for help when they need it, and most important, cry out to God for help? They learn independence and responsibility when we cannot be at their beck and call. This is not a bad thing.

Our response to unreasonable guilt should not be anger. We need to respond to our children with understanding about the root of their frustration, and we must tenderly teach them along life's way. God's Word reminds us to "put away all falsehood and 'tell your neighbor the truth' because we belong to each other. And 'don't sin by letting anger gain control over you,' . . . for anger gives a mighty foothold to the Devil" (Ephesians 4:25–27).

Let's just say your son left his lunch at home, and he lashes out at you when you arrive home that evening, blaming you for working and not being available to bring him his lunch. Instead of reacting by yelling back at him (which would be a huge temptation on any given hormonal day), respond with a teaching moment. "Jonathan, the reason you are angry is that you forgot your lunch and there was no one to cover your error. We all forget things now and then, so we have to compensate—to borrow food or money, or go hungry. We learn responsibility from our mistakes. I bet you won't forget your lunch again."

As we learn to respond to our children in love instead of reacting to them in guilt-driven anger, we begin to change the attitude in the home. Let's face it: Mom usually sets the tone of the home. We have the power to build understanding and acceptance in our families, and we have the power to fuel anger and resentment.

Solomon said, "A wise woman builds her house; a foolish woman tears hers down with her own hands" (Proverbs 14:1). Let's be builders of our homes by our positive responses to the darts of guilt.

Destination: Peace

Our goal is to come to a place of peace with ourselves and with God as to what we are doing and why. For some mothers, it comes down to the reality of financial need. Other mothers work because God has given them an ability, gift, or talent that they know God is leading them to use in the workplace. Who can determine if working outside the home is right for you and your family? We can't answer that question for you. This is a question that must be answered between you and God.

As workingwomen, solid in our resolve, we realize we cannot do it all; so we accept our journey and learn to let go of the baggage. Often we put too much pressure on ourselves to achieve our own impossible image of what we think we were created to be. But our standards are often simply unreasonable. June Cleaver is not real. Martha Stewart has a staff of hundreds to help her create her domestic dynamics. Demi Moore is airbrushed and tweaked by photo imaging on the cover of *Vogue*. But often, we as working mothers think we must achieve this unreachable perfection in our everyday lives.

Shari Thurer, PhD, author of *The Myths of Motherhood: How Culture Reinvents the Good Mother*, says, "Our current ideals of the perfect mom are based on fiction. Or at least not the reality of the 21st century." Thurer adds that highly educated women are "especially prone to working mother guilt because they have been taught that there is a right and a wrong way to approach every situation, when in fact there are many good ways to raise a child."[2]

It's easy to live with the ghost of guilt playing tricks on our minds and echoing the chant, "Need the income, but need to be there for my children. Need the challenge for myself, but need to give to my family too. Not a Type A personality, but live with Type A demands on me. Need to sleep, but need to work late and still have energy to make it through the day."

> Before you begin a thing, remind yourself that difficulties and delays quite impossible to foresee are ahead. . . . You can only see one thing clearly, and that is your goal.
>
> —Kathleen Norris

We must dismiss the garbage and hold on to truth. Proverbs tells us, "A wise person is hungry for truth, while the fool feeds on trash" (Proverbs 15:14). Will we fill our minds with truth or trash? Our attitude really does determine our altitude, so let's focus on the ways God is working through our circumstances, and let's throw away false guilt once and for all.

All moms tend to live with a certain amount of guilt. We continually wonder if we could have done more, done better, or done less. Let's face it: inside or outside the home, we are all working mothers. But positive moms throw away the picture of perfection and find freedom in following God's plan for their lives. The key to peace is not in pleasing everyone or in fulfilling other people's expectations of what a perfect mother ought to be. The key is seeking God's will in all we do and allowing Him to direct our paths (see Proverbs 3:6).

God's Word tells us, "Delight yourself in the LORD and he will give you the desires of your heart. Commit your way to the LORD; trust in him and he will do this" (Psalm 37:4–5 NIV). Our job is to delight in God, to trust Him, and to commit our lives to Him.

God's plan for one woman is not the same as for another. We must walk the path He has set for us. We may struggle with guilt now and then, but we do not have to allow our feelings of guilt to strangle our God-given purpose. Let's pack our bags for the land of peace and confidence and leave the guilt trip behind.

How Are You Coping with Stress?

How well do you sleep?

a. *I fall asleep easily and wake refreshed.*

b. *I sometimes still feel tired in the morning.*

c. *I don't usually sleep through the night.*

d. *I can't stop thinking long enough to fall asleep.*

Which answer best describes your attitude in the morning?

a. *I am usually eager to meet the day.*

b. *It takes a few minutes to mentally prepare myself to meet the day ahead.*

c. *I have to psyche myself up to make it through another day.*

d. *I would rather go back to bed.*

Which of these responses best describes your eating habits?

a. *I consider my appetite to be fairly normal.*

b. *Lately, I find I eat more or less than normal.*

c. *I rarely sit down for a meal.*

d. *Food is a problem area for me.*

How would you describe your physical condition?

a. *I am basically healthy.*

b. *I have a few recurring ailments.*

c. *I seem to be ill much more often lately.*

d. *I never feel completely healthy.*

Which best describes your thought process?

    a. I seem to think clearly most of the time.

    b. I need to stop and organize my thoughts periodically.

    c. I find it difficult to focus on any one thing.

    d. My thoughts are erratic, and my mind feels foggy.

Do you remember things well?

    a. My memory seems as good as ever.

    b. I forget things occasionally.

    c. I seem to require constant reminders.

    d. I can't seem to remember anything lately.

How would you describe a normal day?

    a. I usually accomplish what I set out to do.

    b. My life is hectic, but I am still on top of it.

    c. Too much to do with too little time.

    d. I feel like I am drowning.

Which answer best describes your emotional state?

    a. I am normally on an even keel.

    b. My emotions are a bit unsettled but basically under control.

    c. My emotions are fairly unpredictable.

    d. My emotions are totally out of control.

When you think about tomorrow, do you

    a. Look forward to another day?

    b. Think about all you have to do?

    c. Find yourself getting anxious?

    d. Want to avoid it entirely?

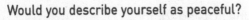

Would you describe yourself as peaceful?

   a. Usually

   b. Sometimes

   c. Rarely

   d. Never

Scoring: Add your points to find your score.

   a = 1 point

   b = 2 points

   c = 3 points

   d = 4 points

10–19: If you scored in this range, you are rare indeed! You deal extremely well with the demands of life and are probably seen by others as well-adjusted and in control.

20–30: If you scored in this range, life is hectic, but you are handling stress fairly well. Focus on what is truly important in life and make sure to keep your priorities in order. Slow down a little, breathe, and face one thing at a time.

31–40: If you scored in this range, your stress level is far too high. It's time to stop and take stock of your life. Some major changes may be called for. High levels of stress can adversely affect your physical and mental health. You may want to speak with your doctor.[3]

The Guilt Factor at a Glance

- Realize that the guilt is there.

- Develop strategies to counteract the guilt.

- Determine if there is anything you can do differently.

- Learn from the challenges.

- Working mothers are good role models.

- Thanks to our example, the next generation of adults will more comfortably combine career and family.

- Remember that your true employer is God.

- Recognize that God uses the rough spots to help you and your children grow.

- Pray and ask God's help and direction.

- Discern false guilt from the real thing.

- Call another working mother to get a clear perspective.

- Respond, but don't react when others make you feel guilty.

• Ask for forgiveness when necessary.

• Realize you can't do it all.

• Identify whom you are trying to please.

• Know and live your priorities.

• Discover the root of the problem.

• Accentuate the positives; eliminate the negatives.

Delete Self-Imposed Guilt with PDA

P—Pray

D—Determine

A—Ask

meditations
for the frazzled soul

If you need wisdom—if you want to know what God wants you to do—ask him, and he will gladly tell you. He will not resent your asking. But when you ask him, be sure that you really expect him to answer, for a doubtful mind is as unsettled as a wave of the sea that is driven and tossed by the wind. People like that should not expect to receive anything from the Lord. They can't make up their minds. They waver back and forth in everything they do.

JAMES 1:5–8

I don't mean to say that I have already achieved these things or that I have already reached perfection! But I keep working toward that day when I will finally be all that Christ Jesus saved me for and wants me to be. No, dear brothers and sisters, I am still not all I should be, but I am focusing all my energies on this one thing: Forgetting the past and looking forward to what lies ahead, I strain to reach the end of the race and receive the prize for which God, through Christ Jesus, is calling us up to heaven.

PHILIPPIANS 3:12–14

Do not fret or have any anxiety about anything, but in every circumstance and in everything, by prayer and petition (definite requests), with thanksgiving, continue to make your wants known to God. And God's peace [shall be yours, that tranquil state of a soul assured of its salvation through Christ, and so fearing nothing from God and being content with its earthly lot of whatever sort that is, that peace] which transcends all understanding shall garrison and mount guard over your hearts and minds in Christ Jesus. For the rest, brethren, whatever is true, whatever is worthy of reverence and is honorable and seemly, whatever is just, whatever is pure, whatever is lovely and lovable, whatever is kind and winsome and gracious, if there is any virtue and excellence, if there is anything worthy of praise, think on and weigh and take account of these things [fix your minds on them.]

PHILIPPIANS 4:6–8 AMP

I rejoice greatly in the Lord that at last you have renewed your concern for me. Indeed, you have been concerned, but you had no opportunity to show it. I am not saying this because I am in need, for I have learned to be content whatever the circumstances. I know what it is to be in need, and I know what it is to have plenty. I have learned the secret of being content in any and every situation, whether well fed or hungry, whether living in plenty or in want. I can do everything through him who gives me strength.

PHILIPPIANS 4:10–13 NIV

If anyone belongs to Christ, there is a new creation. The old things have gone; everything is made new!

2 CORINTHIANS 5:17 NCV

So now, those who are in Christ Jesus are not judged guilty.

ROMANS 8:1 NCV

When you were spiritually dead because of your sins and because you were not free from the power of your sinful self, God made you alive with Christ, and he forgave all our sins. He canceled the debt, which listed all the rules we failed to follow. He took away that record with its rules and nailed it to the cross.

COLOSSIANS 2:13–14 NCV

I, I am the One who forgives all your sins, for my sake; I will not remember your sins.

ISAIAH 43:25 NCV

Advanced parenting techniques

chapter 2

The Parent Factor
Positively Parenting on Purpose

What greater work is there than training the mind
and forming the habits of the young?
St. John Chrysostom

It's just a hunch, but we are going to guess that you have some
sort of career goal or plan for where you want to be five years
from now. If you haven't already written it down, your plans for
the future have at least been rolling around in your head. You may
have a goal of reaching a certain level in your company, or earn-
ing a particular amount of income within the next few years, or
obtaining a certain status. Most of us do think intentionally about
what is down the road and what we need to do to accomplish our
professional goals. As women, we are not typically comfortable
with the prospect of aimlessly wandering through life.

When it comes to our families, women can have a similar,
deliberate focus. Think for a moment about your kids. What do
you hope they will be like five or ten years from now? Describe
them in your mind. What character qualities, value systems, and
manners do you wish they would possess? We're not saying you
are going to force your kids to be something they are not or plan
their future for them. We are saying that our parenting goals can
help us focus on the direction we want our kids to go and the big

picture of life, rather than getting entangled in the small stuff. Fill in the blank space below with the thoughts that come to mind.

My Personal Parenting Goals

It is my hope that my child(ren) will grow to become

_____

_____

_____

_____

You may have found yourself using words like *strong, hardworking, full of integrity, godly, creative, kind,* etc. We all have a mental picture of what we would like to achieve as a parent, but most of us have never verbalized it or put it in writing. Stating our parenting goals is a good, healthy process, don't you agree? But now comes the hardest part. If we know what we would like for our children to become, what path do we take to help them get there?

Dr. Albert Siegel was quoted by the *Stanford Observer* as saying, "When it comes to rearing children, every society is only 20 years away from barbarism. Twenty years is all we have to accomplish the task of civilizing the infants who are born into our midst each year. These savages know nothing of our language, our culture, our religion, our values, and our customs of interpersonal relationships. The barbarian must be tamed if civilization is to survive."[1]

We wouldn't go so far as to call our precious little ones barbarians or savages (although there are times!), but we do concur that, as mothers, we have a big job. A job that requires a goal. A job that demands our attention. It's our job as parents to prepare the next generation for life and to pass on to them our values and standards. As Erma Bombeck said, "There is so much to teach, and the time goes so fast." And Ephesians 5:16 reminds us that we must make the most of our time.

> A bird doesn't sing because it has an answer, it sings because it has a song.
> —Maya Angelou

Let's keep our parenting goals in mind as we proceed through the principles in the rest of the chapter. Our hope is to provide a path for you to reach your goals.

We must also recognize that even though we carefully and prayerfully make our plans, circumstances beyond our control can change the course. Our children's destiny is not in our hands; it is in God's hands. He uses us as parents to teach them, to direct them, and to set them on their way. As we said earlier, our parenting goals are meant to be marks toward which we work, not things we force into reality.

Like a runner with his eyes on the finish line, we want to keep our eyes on our parenting goals, which helps us stay the course and keep on track. When we have goals as to what we want our children to become, it helps us to think long-term and not just about the present. Most important, our parenting goals help us weather the storms that sometimes arise for working mothers.

Parenting 101

How do we effectively teach character and values to our children as we keep our eyes on the goal? Unfortunately there are no Cliffs Notes to perfect parenting, but there are several tried-and-true principles we can apply to our daily lives in order to make an impact on the next generation (or on our little barbarians, as Dr. Siegel called them). Here are three simple strategies that can make a difference in your home.

Teach by Example

Your kids are reading a book every single day. Perhaps you are thinking, *Not my kids; they don't like to read.* Yet we repeat, your kids are reading a book every day! It's called *Life's Living Lessons,* and you are the author! What are some of your chapter titles? "How to Keep Your Cool in Rush-Hour Traffic," "Speaking Kindly Even When You Don't Feel Like It," "Patience in the Checkout Line." Okay, so our chapter titles don't look exactly like that either! The point is, our example to our children speaks louder than words; in fact, at times it shouts. Teaching by our example doesn't take extra time out of our busy schedules. It only takes extra care—extra care to live in a way that you want your kids to live.

It's a little scary as we watch our own children begin to mimic our good and our bad qualities. We each must ask ourselves if our lives exemplify the qualities we want to see in our children. The "do-as-I-say-not-as-I-do" mentality doesn't play out well in our children's lives.

Edgar Guest wrote a powerful poem entitled "Sermons We See," which speaks to the power of our example.

I'd rather see a sermon than hear one any day,
I'd rather one should walk with me than merely show the way.

The eye's a better pupil and more willing than the ear;
Fine counsel is confusing, but example's always clear;

And the best of all the preachers are the men
who live their creeds,
For to see the good in action is what everybody needs.

I can soon learn how to do it if you'll let me see it done.
I can watch your hands in action, but your tongue
too fast may run.

And the lectures you deliver may be very wise and true;
But I'd rather get my lesson by observing what you do.

For I may misunderstand you and the high advice you give,
But there's no misunderstanding how you
act and how you live.

As a case in point, Jackie is a fifteen-year-old gossip. Everyone knows that whatever they tell her will be spread as a juicy story served up on the social round table. How did Jackie become such a gossip? Look no further than her storytelling mom, who savors every delicious morsel of details in other people's lives. Her mom didn't need to teach Jackie the finer points of how to be a malicious gossip. Jackie learned by example.

On the brighter side, consider Aaron, who learned responsibility by observing how his mother handled her work schedule. She did her best to be on time and completed the work projects she was given to the best of her ability. When she made a mistake, she owned up to it (instead of blaming someone else), and if she said she would do something, then she made sure to do it. Aaron grew to be a hardworking, honest, and responsible adult, much to the credit of his mother, whom he watched demonstrate responsibility daily in her work and home life.

Take Advantage of Teachable Moments

Teachable moments—easy, fun, and unplanned insights that we pass on to our kids—are waiting to be discovered. How do we find them? Just look! As you rush through traffic and someone kindly gives you the right of way, point out the driver's kindness to your kids. Teach them that traffic, just like life, flows better when people take the time to be kind to one another.

Even negative experiences can be teachable moments. Take a situation in which a coworker calls you at home and, in a very rude tone, tells you that you have forgotten to do something at the office. You can teach through your example by not reacting to your coworker with anger. You also have the opportunity to teach your kids how it makes you feel when someone is rude to you. You can talk to the kids about how to handle a confrontation in a positive way. And you can use the opportunity to reaffirm to them the importance of responsibility at work as well.

Another teachable moment drops right in our laps at those wonderful moments when our kids have done something wrong and the situation calls for discipline. Punishment and discipline offer an instant teachable moment. Don't miss it! When it comes to discipline, it is good to stick to the three Ds: *dishonesty*, *disrespect*, and *disobedience*. Each family must determine rules in certain gray areas in order to distinguish what matters and what doesn't, but

> The mother's heart is the child's schoolroom.
> —Henry Ward Beecher

the three Ds are unmistakable. If a child is dishonest, disobedient, or disrespectful, then there must be discipline and consequences.

When teachable moments show up in the form of discipline opportunities, remember to communicate the lesson clearly and calmly. Screaming teaches your children nothing except how to scream (hey, we've all been there). Help your kids understand what you expect and describe the right behavior. Teach them why it is important to be honest (or obedient or respectful). Then apply punishment that fits the crime and the child.

Some kids are motivated by money, so taking away allowance is a highly effective form of discipline. Other kids are not money motivated, but they love to watch their favorite shows on television or use the computer, so removing those privileges when the occasion calls for it speaks loudly. Steer away from grounding your child for the next three months, which drags on and on and both of you eventually forget about it. As much as possible, your child's punishment should be short and swift and to the point, helping him or her learn and become a better person through the process.

Plan Devotional Lessons

Now don't worry; we're not talking about long, drawn-out lessons with discussion questions, visual aids, and homework. Planned devotional lessons should be simple. In fact, simple works best. We prefer to use the KISS method—"Keep It Simple, Sister." A planned lesson can come in the form of a family meeting, a dinner-table discussion, or a Saturday morning devotional. It can be weekly, monthly, quarterly, or only on holidays. You must discover what works best for you and your family.

Always be willing to flex and change the way you do planned lessons through the years. What worked for your family when the kids were young may not work so well when they are teenagers. Adjust. When I (Karol) was a teenager, my dad would have family meetings almost every Sunday. He would share with us a short devotional, talk to us about current situations, and pray with us. As for my family, we have found that Monday nights work well for us right now. Currently we read and discuss a chapter from Proverbs. It's simple yet meaningful. We are not always consistent, and we miss a few weeks altogether, but it is something we try to do on a semiregular basis.

You can find wonderful family devotionals at your local Christian bookstore. Our favorites include the following:

Angela Abraham, *Jesus Loves Me Devotional* (Nashville: Tommy Nelson, 2002).

Joyce Vollmer Brown, *Courageous Christians: Devotional Stories for Family Reading* (Chicago: Moody, 2000).

Jean Fischer and Heather Hardison, *Adventures in Odyssey Devotions: Exploring God's Word with Your Adventures in Odyssey Friends* (Nashville: Tommy Nelson, 2000).

Max Lucado and Monica Hall, *Just Like Jesus for Teens* (Nashville: W Publishing, 2003).

Max Lucado, *He Chose You for Teens* (Nashville: W Publishing, 2002).

Dandi Daley Mackall, *Kids Say the Best Things about Life: Devotions and Conversations for Families on the Go* (San Francisco: Jossey-Bass, 2004).

Frank E. Peretti, *Wild and Wacky Totally True Bible Stories* (Nashville: Tommy Nelson, 2002).

Joe White, *Fuel: 10-Minute Devotions to Ignite the Faith of Parents and Teens* (Wheaton, Ill.: Tyndale, 2003).

Bruce H. Wilkinson, ed., *Family Walk* (Grand Rapids: Zondervan, 1991).

Bruce H. Wilkinson and Rob Suggs, *The Prayer of Jabez: Devotions for Kids Living Big for God* (Nashville: Tommy Nelson, 2001).

Tom Ziegler and Lori Ziegler, eds., *As for Me and My House: 50 Easy-to-Use Devotionals for Families* (Woburn, Mass.: Discipleship Publications, 2003).

While growing up, my (Jane's) family had a short devotional and a prayer time together each night before bed. If my dad was out of town, my mom would lead the time. The devotional time was not long and drawn out, no one took an offering or sang six verses of "Just as I Am," but it was a time for connecting spiritually. It was also a time for acknowledging that the heavenly Father was the One who directed our lives. As for my family now, we have family night once a week. Sunday night consists of pizza and a movie, then a time of devotional reading, prayer, and discussion.

Heart Matters

Strategies are well and good, but the most important thing we can do as mothers is to make a heart connection with our children. It is easy to want our kids to look great on the outside, yet the real issues of character lie beneath the surface level. Whether we are disciplining our kids or talking to them about life choices, we want to get to the heart of the matter.

Children are real. They have remarkably clear thought patterns, and sometimes their thoughts are peppered with brutal honesty. The refreshing part is that they have yet to learn or see the point of being any other way. The fog of other people's opinions or social expectations has yet to be learned. In fact, if you need an honest opinion, ask a five-year-old! A child will tell you just what he or she is thinking.

In Brenda Waggoner's book *The Velveteen Woman*, she explains realness like this: "Real is something we become gradually, as we face life vulnerably, returning to God over and over and finding ourselves loved, even when life hurts, when it doesn't make sense, when we are angry or afraid."[3] As mothers, we must first be real ourselves, then pass that trait on to our children.

> There is no influence so powerful as that of a mother.
> —Sarah J. Hale

We do not need to be afraid to let our kids see our flaws. It's okay for them to see that we can't do it all and be it all. Our children don't need a perfect mom; they need a real one. A real mom says, "I am not able to meet all of your needs and to be there for you 100 percent of the time, but God can." Through our humility, our kids can sense a genuine love.

Genuine love, the kind described in 1 Corinthians 13 (see the end of this chapter), doesn't come naturally. It's not always easy to be patient and kind, not rude or irritable. It's not always easy to listen and care and get to the heart of a matter. So how do we love with a genuine love? The Bible says that "love comes from God" (1 John 4:7). His love is perfect, kind, patient, and thoughtful. Although we may not have the capacity to demonstrate pure love on our own, we can ask God to pour His precious love through us to our family. When we recognize how wonderful God's love is toward us, and ask Him to pour His love through us, we can be confident that He will do it.

Compassion is another heart issue that is at the center of an authentic and Christlike life. In Psalm 103:8, David says, "The LORD is compassionate and gracious" (NIV). Since we were created to bring glory to God by becoming more and more like Him, compassion for others is a necessary ingredient for our recipe of life. Compassion is more than sympathy. Sympathy feels sorry; compassion takes feeling sorry the extra mile by showing a desire to help and acting on that desire to make a certain situation better.

As co-leader of her daughter's Brownie troop, Diane never knew what to expect. Last week as fourteen eight-year-old girls

> Whatever the times, one thing will never change: Fathers and mothers, if you have children, they must come first. Your success as a family, our success as a society, depends not on what happens in the White House, but what happens inside your house.
>
> —Barbara Bush

and their leaders were looking for birds indigenous to Texas, they had quite a fright. Little did she know that three eight-year-old boys were spying on the troop as the girls diligently worked to complete their Earth and Sky badges.

The spy kids were spotted when one of the boys began screaming. Apparently he had jumped from one side of the creek to the other, landing on a filthy stick that lodged straight into his leg. The look on his face was sheer agony. The bird watchers froze. Diane looked quickly at the boy's injury, scooped him up, and ran up and over the creek to his house. His father took him to the emergency room.

They continued their Brownie meeting after attempting to answer the barrage of questions from the inquisitive young ladies. As they closed, one very compassionate Brownie member came over and whispered in her ear, "Miss Diane, can we make him a get-well card and sign it from all the Brownies?" "Of course," Diane replied. And they did, each girl writing her own condolences, filled with empathy for a young boy whose spying had backfired.

When the injured boy and his family returned later that evening from the hospital, a beautiful, handmade, love-filled card awaited their arrival. Why? Because of the kindness put into action by one young girl. Compassion is a lot like bird-watching: you have to be looking to capitalize on the opportunity to share.

How do we develop compassion in young hearts?

• Be an example of compassion to our children.

• Role-play certain situations in which compassion would be just the ticket to mend hurt feelings.

- Share Bible stories in which the characters showed compassion to another.

- Share a time in your life when someone showed compassion to you.

One of the most important heart issues we can encourage in our kids is a healthy fear of the Lord. By fear of the Lord, we mean a reverence and respect for God. Proverbs 9:10 tells us the "fear of the LORD is the beginning of wisdom." A reverence for God inspires us to live a life of integrity, extend the hand of compassion, and reach out with forgiveness to others. Most important, a healthy fear of the Lord leads us to God's Word and to the message of Christ. Proverbs is a wonderful place to start when it comes to teaching the fear of the Lord to our children.

We teach our kids a healthy fear of the Lord as we demonstrate it in our own lives. As our kids see us bow our knees to pray, give back something that doesn't belong to us, or demonstrate self-control in our language, they begin to pick up on the fact that we reverence God and our fellowman. Fearing God also means that we humbly recognize our need for Him. We know that we have sinned and come short of God's glory, as the Bible says in Romans 3:23. That's why He sent His Son, Jesus, to pay the penalty for our sin. How glorious that fear of the Lord leads us to the cross of Christ. Through our words and example, may we be faithful to teach our children a healthy fear of our great God.

Practical Parenting

As much as we would love for parenting to be all about meaningful lessons and life-changing experiences, the truth is that there are day-to-day struggles. Let's address some of the unique challenges for a working mom and look at positive solutions to help you through.

Finding Regular Childcare

Finding the right childcare program is essential to your peace of mind as a working mom. As you check out childcare options in your area, we suggest you call local churches and network with other mothers before making your decision. Many churches offer excellent day-care programs that provide spiritual education and godly love. Word of mouth can be the greatest advertisement when it comes to childcare programs. Ask at the playground, at work, and at church to find which programs are "mother-pleasing" programs.

Here are some questions to ask and tips to use when interviewing a potential day-care provider for your kids:

- Tell me how you started in the day-care/childcare business. How long have you been in business? What are your credentials and qualifications?

- How do you handle discipline issues?

- What is your procedure for sick children?

- What is your daily routine for the kids (playtime, snacks, lunch, nap)?

- For infant care, is there a way to monitor my baby's development and skills?

- Do you take the children on field trips or places outside this facility? If so, what type of transportation is used?

- Inquire about specific issues that concern you and your family (such as toilet training, snacks, nap time, medications, etc.).

- Ask for references and then check the references.

- Inquire about cleanliness and how well the facility is cleaned and sanitized.

- Walk around the facility and look at the other children and workers in action.

- Pray and ask the Lord to give you discernment and wisdom. Ask Him to alert you to any red flags.

Remember, this is one of your most important decisions as a working mother. Take time and care to make a wise decision.

Caring for a Sick Child

Perhaps the biggest challenge of a working mom is determining what to do if your child is sick. The first and best choice for taking care of a sick child in the midst of your work responsibilities is to have a workable plan with many options.

Here are a few tips to help you make a master plan. For more tips, go to the National Association for Sick Child Daycare web site: www.nascd.com.

- *Create a "backup posse."* Ask trusted family members or friends who are typically available during your work time to be available in case of sickness or emergency. Have more than one option, since nobody wants to create a wedge in a strong relationship by calling just when trouble is looming. Consider fellow church members, elderly neighbors, or local college students as resources to add to this list. Look for people who have a flexible schedule.

- *Alternate time off with your husband.* If you are married, the parent with more flexibility is the point person when sickness hits the household. Alternate the time missed from work with your husband.

- *Register for sick-child care.* Many large day-care centers are offering sick-child care in addition to regular day care. This option typically includes a comfortable room and bed and lots of tender, loving care. Most require early registration for this option, so don't wait until sickness hits to arrange for this great backup plan. Few babysitters or home day-care centers offer this service unless your doctor writes a note stating that your child has a noncontagious illness.

- *Take your work home.* Address your sick-child work options with your employer before the situation arises. If your child is sick, will you be allowed to work from home that day? This adds security for both parties.

- *Find a family-friendly workplace.* Consider bosses with

children and workplaces that honor the importance of family when selecting a place to send a résumé.

Arranging Transportation and Carpools

It seems at times that a mom's biggest job description is chauffeur. Getting our kids to and from school, practices, and meetings can be a daunting task. What do you do when your work and family transportation schedule just don't seem to synchronize? Here are some ways to make sure your kids get where they need to be when you need to be at work.

Check with your children's school system to see if they have early-morning or after-school programs.

Many local churches offer after-school pickup programs. Check with neighborhood churches; if they don't have one, ask if they will start one (be proactive for all the working moms out there!).

Consider neighborhood friends whom your children can go home with on a regular basis. Agree to compensate the other parents. Consider rotating different friends on different days of the week. Again, make sure you know the friends well. Your children will become like the people they hang around.

Hire a high-school or college student to help you transport your kids. Make sure he or she is a responsible and respected young adult with high moral standards. Your kids may love having the opportunity to be around older kids, and they can be a positive influence and example for your children.

If you have older kids, you must carefully plan how they will be supervised after school or with whom they will be "hanging out." The hours between school's final bell and a parent's arrival back from work is typically a time when kids can get into trouble, so make sure you know your child's friends or arrange for some form of accountability.

Handling Homework

Homework can become a challenging task not only for our kids, but for us as working moms. Here are some creative yet easy tips on how to help your children through their homework woes.

- *Talk to your child's teachers.* Early in the school year, respectfully ask your child's teacher or teachers how much time they expect students to budget for homework each night. Asking ahead will give you time to create a plan that works best for your family.

- *Stay in touch with their teachers.* Most teachers prefer e-mail.

- *Use your multitasking skills.* Create a space close to the kitchen for your children to do their homework. This gives you the option of cooking dinner while they study. You are close should questions arise, but you can accomplish your work too.

- *Design your best homework routine.* The American Academy of Pediatrics recommends "a positive homework atmosphere free of clutter and distractions, including television." Having a set time and place to do homework will pay off in less procrastination, complaining, and late-night rushes.

- *Organize assignments.* Post a calendar on which due dates can be marked, and teach your children project-management skills. Do you demonstrate good organizational and time-management skills, or do your kids see you scrambling to do a big project the night before it's due? Make it each child's responsibility to bring an assignment folder or list home each night.

- *Don't do your kids' homework for them.* In the homework arena, we should act as a guide but not provide. Be available to answer your children's questions, but do not do the work for them.

- *Work first; play later.* Encourage your kids to maximize their schoolwork time, allowing for more time with friends later. If they're busy passing notes or talking to their neighbors in study hall, then the natural consequence is for them to bring the work home. Time with friends or family (playtime for younger kids, phone or mall time for older ones) can be the reward after the homework is done.

- *Use online resources to help with homework.* There are dozens of web sites that can help your children with their homework, such as www.eduhound.com and www.americaslibrary.gov. Just be sure that you are able to monitor your children's use of the Internet, either by personally supervising their computer time or by installing a reliable Internet filter, such as Bsafe Online (available at www.bsafeonline.com).

Flying Solo

In the realm of relationships, our lives can change drastically, sometimes due to circumstances beyond our control. For a multitude of different reasons, you may find yourself parenting by yourself. You may be a single parent, or you may have a spouse who is out of town or away from home a great deal, making you a single parent for the majority of the time. If you are in the role of a single parent, we want to offer you a helping hand and a hopeful outlook. You will find that one of the first steps to single-parenting success is surrounding yourself with the right people.

In her book *No More Lone Ranger Moms*, author and mother Donna Partow offers these thoughts: "This motherhood trip wasn't designed for lone rangers. It takes more than one woman against the world to raise a child in this increasingly complex and dangerous world. Even the pioneers sometimes circled the wagons. Women need one another. It's time to circle the wagons."[4]

Carefully crafting your "parenting posse" can be the beginning of the hope and help you need. Here are some ideas for pulling together with other people in order to circle up those wagons.

- *Find a baby-sitting co-op.* Check local newsletters, neighborhood associations, church groups, or newspapers to see if there are any co-ops available near you. A baby-sitting co-op basically allows you to trade baby-sitting responsibilities or hours with another parent. You may find that it is quite easy to start one in your work or neighborhood community. Consider the people you know who are home during the day or who have flexible hours. Perhaps you know someone with whom you might trade baby-sitting services in exchange for something you can do, such as legal work, typing, cleaning, or mending.

• *Join an encouragement or support group.* By joining with other single moms, you can strengthen one another and find the solace and sympathy you need to make it through another day. One group of single mothers in our area started a once-a-month encouragement group for moms. They decided they would not get together to gripe; rather, they get together to build each other up and support each other. Often they eat together, hear a speaker, and then break up into small groups to pray for each other. One month a massage therapist gave the women massages. During the holidays, they asked a psychologist to talk about handling the holidays as a single parent. They also exchange phone numbers and contact information so they can be available to one another. If you cannot find a group like this in your area, consider starting one. E-mail us information about your group so that we can connect other mothers in your area through our web site: www.HighHeelsandHomeLife.com.

• *Build a support group online.* Share e-mail with other working moms to create an online working-mother support group. When the kids are in bed and you have a free moment, you can ask questions, share prayer requests, and offer a word of encouragement to one another.

- *Keep open lines of communication with the children's father.* Ask the Lord for guidance, kindness, and discernment when it comes to issues with the father. Although things may never be as they once were, working together as much as possible can be helpful and healing to the children.

- *Connect with godly men in your area.* It is helpful to connect with supportive, godly men in your community for a number of reasons. They can offer mentoring to your son(s), help with a decision, or assist around the house. Some churches offer male support for single moms. You may find it helpful to seek out a retired man who has the time to help in certain areas and would be happy to give his time.

Building community with other working moms who share the same values and focus will offer tremendous assistance while you are striving to meet the demands of work and home. Don't try to do it all on your own. Connect with others in support and strength. Remember, God is with you always. At times when you feel alone, take a moment to look to Him and ask for His help and warm embrace.

Daddy Dearest

It takes two to tango, right? Well, it may take two to tango, but there are times when most of the parenting responsibilities fall squarely on the shoulders of the mother. Is it proper to expect a dad to assist? In a two-income family, the answer should be yes. But just how do we best communicate this? How do we define the parenting roles when our parents may not have modeled them for us?

Seven Ways to Get Your Husband to Help with the Children

- Tell him that you appreciate his help.

- Explain how his help will benefit the children and you.

- Motivate him by showing enthusiasm.

- Encourage him with kind words.

- Ask him to plan a father-son day or a father-daughter date.

- Reward your husband by cooking his favorite dinner.

- Support his leadership . . . especially in front of the children.

(Source: Laurie Whaley and Beverly Riggs, eds., *Becoming*, NCV Bible (Nashville: Thomas Nelson, 2004), 303.)

First, take a good, long look at your parenting expectations. Expectations that do not mesh with reality become a breeding ground for discontent. Discontent can color your world in shades you never thought possible. If you find your home life to be less than satisfactory, stop and reflect on this area of your relationship with your husband with these questions:

Which portrayal fits you?

_____ 50-50 partner with my husband

_____ 100 percent responsible for parenting, with my
husband as helper

_____ Helper to my husband, who is 100 percent
responsible for parenting

While there are many other possible options, these questions reveal a bit about our thinking. Where do you think the responsibility of parenting should lie in your marriage? What does your view of the style of your husband's fathering say about your respect for him? How can you get the most from your parenting partnership?

With this in mind, let's take a deliberate look at your parenting expectations.

Name five ways you and your husband parent similarly.

_____

_____

_____

_____

_____

Now name five ways you and your husband parent differently.

_____

_____

_____

_____

Name three specific ways you can celebrate the differences in personality and parenting styles you've just identified.[5]

_____

_____

_____

Realizing where we are in our parenting journey helps us align our expectations with our reality when it comes to dividing responsibilities with our spouses. Here are a few tips to offer hope in our parenting pursuit.

Developing a co-parenting style requires honest self-examination and conscious communication. Both parents must feel a shared sense of ownership for and responsibility to the well-being of your children and the family unit as a whole. Take time to sit down with your husband (preferably over dinner at a nice restaurant) and consider the following ideas to help your parenting partnership succeed. Don't force any or all of these ideas on him. Instead, open up the discussion and communicate with confidence and kindness.

- *Establish a monthly "state of the union" address.* Communicate with your husband what is working, what is not, and how life can be smoothed for the family.

- *Communicate expectations clearly and directly.* For example, he does the yard work; you do the housework; he takes out the trash; you pay the bills.

- *Pray together for the kids and for your marriage.* Ask God to continue to guide you and strengthen you as a family.

- *Divide the responsibilities in an equitable manner,* according to both of your gifts, talents, and natural bents. Don't divide responsibilities according to who makes the most money but rather by who has the most demands on his or her time and who has the most flexible schedule.

- *Be open to change.* If parenting patterns need to change in your family, be prepared to take the risk to help them change.

- *Plan to redistribute responsibilities.* Work out a system if you need your spouse to take over some of your responsibilities.

- *Give more than you feel as though you are receiving.* Things will never be perfectly fair, and it will always seem like you are doing more (though your husband will typically think he is doing more). Take on a servant's heart and remind yourself that it is okay to do more than your fair share in your family. We are never so Christlike as when we are dying to self and serving others.

- *Create a family calendar.* On the first of each month, you and your husband each take a look at your calendars, along with the kids' school calendars and extracurricular activities. Compile all important information into a family calendar. Plan who is driving where and attending what in order to reduce any last-minute crisis situations.

If necessary, pay for help. If you and your husband simply aren't able to adjust your schedules so that one of you can be home with the children, arrange in advance for appropriate childcare. Or if you can't squeeze in time for housework or yard work, consider hiring help for those areas.

Staying Connected with Your Kids

Ultimately the challenge of working moms is to stay connected with our kids, no matter what their ages. When you reunite with your children after work and school, remember these three words: *look, listen,* and *touch.* These three simple words can help deepen your connection with your family.

Look them in the eyes. In other words, don't be so busy reading the mail or feeding the dog that you don't see them and connect through eye contact.

Listen to them. You may not be able to listen to everything each child has to say about his or her day, but you can take a moment to really hear your child. Turn off the phone and television, and take a few minutes to focus on your children. Ask them an open-ended question, such as, "Tell me something good that happened to you today." Then be all ears as you listen to the response.

Touch each child by hugging, kissing, or holding hands. It seems so simple, but often in the busy bustle of daily life, we overlook the power of our touch. A gentle backrub as they tell you about their day can be a wonderful way for your kids to open up to you.

Here are some practical tips that will help you stay connected with your children:

- *Never underestimate the power of a note.* Write a short but sweet expression of encouragement on a sticky

note for each of your kids as you leave work, then put
the notes on their mirror or homework when you get
home. E-mail them from work and let them know
how special they are to you.

• *Encourage your children often.* The word *encourage*
means to give strength. Give strength to your kids ver-
bally as often as you can. Be sincere and be specific.
Tell them what you see in them and what you know
they can do. Compliment them on the kind deeds they
do and the integrity they show. A good word costs so
little, but its value is priceless.

• *Smile.* It doesn't take a great deal of time or effort, but
a smile speaks a thousand words. A smile is a precious
gift you give your children. When you smile at your
children, you communicate, "I love you. I'm proud of
you. You're going to make it." Even if you don't feel like
smiling, give a smile to your kids and the feeling will
follow. Remember, a smile is not for you; it is for them.

• *Share their emotions.* Although we just mentioned smiling, it is important for us to mention that there is a time
to smile and there is a time to cry. In the Bible we read,
"When others are happy, be happy with them. If they are
sad, share their sorrow" (Romans 12:15). When your
child is sad about something, be sad with him or her (if
it is appropriate). There will be a time and a place later
to share the lighter side and tell them that things will get
better. First, let them know that you feel their pain.

- *Start a "devotional-on-the-run."* Using a journaling note-book, write a Bible verse at the top of a page each night before you go to sleep. In the morning, set out the notebook and tell your children that they each need to read the Bible verse and make a comment about it in the notebook. It is wonderful to read back over your children's entries.

Five Essentials of Discipline

- Communicate to your children what you expect.

- Maintain consistent boundaries.

- Present a united front.

- Consider the personality factor: what works for one child may not work for another.

- Make the punishment fit the crime.

(Source: Jane Jarrell, *Mom Matters* (Eugene, Ore.: Harvest House, 2000), 38.)

The bottom line in parenting as a working mom is to keep the big picture in mind. Take a look at your parenting goals once again and recognize that, although there will be some challenges along the way, there are only a few issues that matter in the big scheme of life. Pass on to your children the values that truly are important through your example and your words. And remember, don't just scratch the surface, but get to the heart of your child through genuine love, the kind of love God has for us. With His help, we can parent with confidence. Remember, you are not alone.

The Parent Factor at a Glance

• Teach your children by example. Life's lessons are often caught, not taught.

• Discover teachable moments. They are everywhere.

• Plan devotional lessons. Use the KISS method—"Keep It Simple, Sister." Share truths with your family over breakfast, in the car, or right before bed.

• Administer discipline when your children commit one of the three Ds: dishonesty, disrespect, or disobedience.

• Nurture your children from the inside out. Focus on inner beauty rather than outer glam.

• Be real. Fake's a mistake; real is the deal.

• Practice compassion. Love others as Christ first loved us.

• Always keep the big picture of your parenting goals in mind.

• Create a parenting posse to help you.

• Determine how your style of parenting differs from your husband's—and appreciate the differences.

• Never underestimate the power of a handwritten note.

• Listen to your children and your spouse with your whole heart.

• Turn off the phone and television during your special time with your children.

• Create your own workable "devotional-on-the-run" ideas.

meditations
for the frazzled soul

Love the LORD your God with all your heart and with all your soul and with all your strength. These commandments that I give you today are to be upon your hearts. Impress them on your children. Talk about them when you sit at home and when you walk along the road, when you lie down and when you get up.

DEUTERONOMY 6:5–7 NIV

Train a child in the way he should go, and when he is old he will not turn from it.

PROVERBS 22:6 NIV

Be kind and compassionate to one another, forgiving each other, just as in Christ God forgave you.

EPHESIANS 4:32 NIV

Love is patient and kind. Love is not jealous or boastful or proud or rude. Love does not demand its own way. Love is not irritable, and it keeps no record of when it has been wronged. It is never glad about injustice but rejoices whenever the truth wins out. Love never gives up, never loses faith, is always hopeful, and endures through every circumstance.

1 CORINTHIANS 13:4–7

Dear friends, let us continue to love one another, for love comes from God.

1 JOHN 4:7

chapter 3

The Relationship Factor

Developing Meaningful Relationships in the Fast Lane

Warmth, kindness, and friendship are the most
yearned for commodities in the world. The person who
can provide them will never be lonely.

—ANN LANDERS

Have you had the opportunity to meet Mr. Wonderful? Actually,
you can purchase him for around ten dollars at a local drugstore.
So what makes Mr. Wonderful so wonderful? It all comes down
to what he says. Simply push the little button on his shirt, and
you'll hear him say one of the following phrases:

- "Here, you take the remote. As long as I'm with you, I don't care what we watch."

- "You know, honey, why don't you just relax and let me make dinner tonight."

- "Actually I'm not sure which way to go. I'll turn in here and ask for directions."

- "Aw, can't your mother stay another week?"

- "The ball game isn't really that important. I'd rather spend time with you."

- "Let's just cuddle tonight."

If only relationships were that easy! Perhaps a better name for Mr. Wonderful would be Fiction Man. But we can't say too much here, because the same company that created the Mr. Wonderful doll also came up with Ms. Wonderful. Here's what she has to say:

- "Don't worry about taking the trash out; I can use the exercise."

- "It really doesn't matter if you leave the toilet seat up; it makes it easier to clean."

- "A new reversible drill—oh, honey, it's just what I needed!"

- "You're going out with the boys tonight? You've worked hard. Enjoy yourself."

- "Oh, you're watching the ball game. Just stay right there on the couch and I'll whip up some snacks."

- "I'll finish cleaning out the garage, honey. Your friends are waiting for you to play golf."[1]

Oh well, no one's perfect. And that's just it! No one is perfect. We all have flaws and weaknesses, and we all make mistakes. It's those imperfections that make relationships a little more difficult to cultivate and grow. If we were all Mr. or Ms. Wonderful, then relating to one another wouldn't be an issue. (But life would be a little boring, don't you think?)

Developing meaningful relationships may not be easy, but it is one of the most fulfilling pursuits we can undertake. When Jesus gave the Great Commandment, He summed up all the commands of God in two simple steps: love God and love others. At the end of our lives, it is not the money that we made or the awards that we received that will be important. The most important aspect of our lives will be our relationship with God and our relationships with the people He placed around us.

In his best-selling book *The Friendship Factor,* author Alan Loy McGinnis acknowledges that in order to experience genuine friendships, we must make love a priority. He goes on to say:

> As I watched those who are deeply loved, I've noticed they all believe that people are a basic source of happiness. Their companions are very important to them, and no matter how busy their schedule, they have developed a life-style and a way of dispensing their time that allows them to have several profound relationships with people.
>
> On the other hand, in talking to lonely persons I often discover that, though they lament their lack of close companions, they actually place little emphasis on the cultivation of friends. Like Howard Hughes, they are so occupied earning money, acquiring degrees, or building their stamp collections, that they do not have time to let love grow.[2]

In this chapter we want to explore ways that we as working moms can develop and deepen the relationships in our lives.

Despite our busy schedules, making and developing loving relationships with others can still be a priority. We recognize that life is more meaningful when we enjoy it with those we love, so we want to offer ways to enhance not only our marriage and family relationships, but our friendships as well.

First Comes Love

Sydney, a mother of three, recounts the ebb and flow of her marriage as follows:

> A long walk down a beautiful beach at sunset is the perfect backdrop for falling in love. Lapping waves, sea gulls flying overhead, a gentle breeze wafting through your hair. This is the ideal kindling for igniting the fire of love. That's how my husband, Matt, and I began our life together, Mr. and Mrs Wonderful. Then we snapped out of it. Life hit us, with its real problems, real struggles—and there was no beach for miles.
>
> First comes love, and I suppose that's a good thing, because all that comes after the first love tests our commitment. We started with nothing, and often I wonder if we'll end with nothing. We've had a consistent financial strain, barely enough money to make ends meet. It takes its toll. Will we make it to the finish line? I look to God for those answers, renew my thoughts and vows, and keep at it. [5]

Relationships, and especially marriages, can be difficult. Relationships take work, persistence, and a tenacious attitude.

Sydney goes on to say that the secret of her healthy marriage is "our commitment to God first and then to each other."

Are relationships worth striving for? As much as we may want to think we can go it alone or do things independently, we were created as relational beings. Even in the Garden of Eden, where all creation was perfect, there was one thing that was not good. It was not good that man was alone, so God created a companion for him. Whether you are married or single, you need good friends in your life to sharpen you and to nourish you. Friends truly are a gift from God.

Wise Solomon put it this way: "Two are better than one, because they have a good return for their work: If one falls down, his friend can help him up. But pity the man who falls and has no one to help him up!" (Ecclesiastes 4:9–10 NIV). The apostle Paul also spoke of the importance of community and working together, everyone using their gifts and talents for the body of Christ (see Romans 12:4–8; 1 Corinthians 12). Even Christ Himself knew the blessings of having close friends by His side in time of need. You may remember that when Jesus was in the Garden of Gethsemane preparing to face His final hour, He asked His closest companions to stay with Him and pray (see Matthew 26:36).

We all need friends by our sides not only in times of need but also in times of joy. Life's greatest moments are best enjoyed with a friend. In his book *When All You've Ever Wanted Isn't Enough*, Harold Kushner says, "A life without people, without the same people day after day, people who belong to us, people who will be there for us, people who need us and whom we need in return, may be very rich in other things, but in human terms, it is no life at all."[4]

Practical Priorities

You may be thinking, *That is all well and good for you, but how in the world can I make relationships a priority between work and kids? Who has the time?*

What if we told you that making relationships a priority isn't a time-drainer? The main thing it takes is intentional thought. Making and developing relationships with others is an attitude and way of life more than it is a time-grabbing activity. We want to let you in on seven secrets to deepening the current and potential relationships in your life.

Where did we get these secrets? Over the past ten years, we have spoken at numerous women's meetings and retreats. As we have examined the friendships and relationships of women, certain relational principles have continually surfaced. Considering these principles, we have compiled seven significant and lasting truths about how women relate to each other. As you intentionally apply these principles to your life, you will see that when you make relationships a priority in your heart and mind, you can work on them even in the daily, busy routine of your life.

Developing better relationships doesn't come down to a less busy lifestyle. There are plenty of people who have a great deal of time on their hands, yet they still struggle with relationships. No, more free time is not necessarily the answer. Would being better organized with our time increase our relationships? If that were the case, we would send you each a Day-Timer and give you a time-management seminar so you would be

> There
> is no possession
> more valuable
> than a good and
> faithful friend.
> —Socrates

62

a better friend to others. But better time management doesn't necessarily result in more meaningful relationships. Although we do need to be careful of filling up our schedules to the brim, we can still learn how to have wonderful, dynamic relationships within our current life-

> A true friend is the gift of God, and he who made hearts can untie them.
> —Robert South

style. It all comes down to a saying you have heard all of your life (and may have said repeatedly to your own children): "If you want to have friends, you must learn to be a friend."

That's what this chapter is all about: being a good friend. We want to share with you seven basic principles for being a good friend to the people around you—at home and at work. As you take on these traits, you will begin to see a difference in your relationships.

Before we give you the seven secrets, we want to encourage you to think about ways to apply them. First, consider the people in your life. Generally speaking, these people fall into one of three categories: acquaintances, good friends, and soul mates.

Acquaintances are those people you know but don't know well. You may or may not know their names. Your conversations with acquaintances are usually surface level and short. Included in this group are coworkers, people who work at retail establishments you frequent, people at church, parents of children who are in the same class or participate in the same activities as yours, and neighbors. Depending on your personality, you may have between twenty to two hundred acquaintances.

From that pool of acquaintances come those people with whom you recognize you have a connection. You have an "aha" moment, when you turn to each other and realize, "Oh, you see it that way, and so do I!" Thus, a friendship is born. Good friends, or kindred spirits, are those people in your life with whom you get past the surface fluff. You talk about ideas and interests, opinions, and possibly even politics. You could have five to twenty-five good friends in your life at one time. Good friends may come and go, and some will grow into that closest of relationships known as soul mates.

Soul mates, or heart-to-heart friends, are those close friends with whom you can share not only your opinions, but also your hopes, dreams, and disappointments. Your spouse should be in this category, but unfortunately for most of us, our spouses have become merely acquaintances in the fast lane of life. We need to bring our spouses back into the soul mate category. Soul mates are people with whom we connect on the deepest level. Consider yourself blessed if you have even three or four soul mates in your entire lifetime.

Even if you haven't talked with your soul mate friend in months, you have the kind of connection that can pick up right where you left off. You know each other and understand each other. Soul mate friendships are the most meaningful relationships in life. Our goal isn't to have the most acquaintances in life; our goal in relationships is to have connection.

The point of these seven secrets of meaningful relationships is to bring acquaintances into the circle of good friends, and eventually some will become soul mates. The seven secrets will help you deepen the relationships you already have in your life. These secrets are not only meant for friendships, but they are also meant to enhance your marriage or dating relationships. You may also find them helpful to pass along to your kids as they grow and mature in their friendship circles.

Seven Secrets of Finding and Deepening Relationships

Secret #1:
Take a Genuine Interest in Other People

In his book *How to Win Friends and Influence People*, Dale Carnegie said, "You can gain more friends in two months by taking a genuine interest in other people than you can in two years trying to get people interested in you."[5] How do you begin to take a genuine interest in others? We believe it begins with looking and listening.

Look at the people around you—your kids, your coworkers, people in your building at work, customers, clients. Have you really seen them, or do you simply pass them by as you go through the motions at work and at home? Look at each person as if he or she has an invisible sign around the neck that reads "I want to feel important." Every person is a treasure chest full of gems. Each person around us has gifts and stories and feelings that are waiting to be discovered. Yet we often only see glaring annoyances and overlook the fact that each person offers something valuable to this world. Look for the value in every person you encounter.

Listen—we mean really listen—to others. Do you hear what they are saying, or do you simply hear their words? Ask questions that attempt to draw out some of those gems. Think more about ways to find out about others rather than trying to let them know about you.

To those at work:

- "Oh, is that a picture of your kids? What are their ages? Tell me about them."

- "I noticed you were gone last week. Were you on vacation? Where did you go?"

- "How was your weekend? Did you do anything special?"

- "Where is your favorite place for lunch around here?"

To those at home:

- "How was your day? Tell me one thing you did today that you enjoyed."

- "You seem like you are in a good mood. Is there something that happened today that was good?"

- "You seem a little bothered. Is everything all right?"

As we look at every person who touches our daily lives and really see them and listen to them, we begin to see the treasures of their hearts being revealed. This is how we develop a deeper connection and grow closer to others. The Bible tells us, "Don't think only about your own affairs, but be interested in others, too, and what they are doing" (Philippians 2:4). Your attitude should be the same that Christ Jesus had. When Jesus lived on this earth, He was continually thinking of others, reaching out to them, and really seeing them. Let's follow His example as we encounter the people He brings along our path each day.

Secret #2: Be Loyal

Loyalty is a rare commodity in today's world. An old Turkish proverb says, "He is loyal to one friend, thus proves himself worthy of many." Are you loyal to your friends behind their backs? Are you consistently there for them? Loyalty doesn't mean that a friend stays as a close friend for the rest of your life. Friendships cycle in and out of our lives in a very natural way. But loyalty means we won't stab people in the back while pretending to their faces that they are still our friends.

Loyalty takes courage. We must have strength and integrity mixed together to guard our mouths when we know something we could add to a juicy story. We don't have to tell everything we know, especially if it is at the expense of another. Often people want the cheap reward of smut conversation, and they will say anything about anyone to engage in this sort of slander. Gossip is a killer to relationships; loyalty is a builder. Never tell another person's story, but rather gain a reputation of trust that people can count on.

A gossiper or storyteller may appear to have friends, but what they really have is conversations. Who can trust a person who tells stories? We all know that if a friend is telling us malicious stories about other people, they are also telling other people malicious stories about us. It happens every time. A gossip cannot be trusted, but a loyal friend is a trustworthy friend.

Secret #3: Be a Giver, Not a Taker

Ask not what your friend can do for you, but rather what you can do for your friend. What can you give to your friend? A listening ear, an encouraging word, help at work, a smile, a hug, or a quick note. Giving doesn't take as much time as it takes attention.

> We make a living by what we get, but we make a life by what we give.
> —Winston Churchill

The reward of relationships is not what you can get out of people but rather what you can give to them.

Jesus said there is a return for giving kindness. As He spoke to His followers in what we now call the Sermon on the Mount, Jesus said, "Give, and it will be given to you. A good measure, pressed down, shaken together and running over, will be poured into your lap. For with the measure you use, it will be measured to you" (Luke 6:38 NIV). You have probably heard this verse in a sermon about money, but in the context, Jesus was talking about kindness, love, and forgiveness.

Kindness, love, and forgiveness are the commodities with which we need to be generous to others, not stingy. Now before we go on, take a moment to examine the relationships in your life and answer the following questions in your heart:

- Is there someone in your life from whom you are holding back kindness?

- Is there someone who needs to see your love demonstrated in words or actions?

- Is there a friend or loved one from whom you have withheld forgiveness?

Ouch! That last one is a tough one. Forgiveness isn't easy, but as Christians we are called to forgive. Why? Christ forgave us of everything, so what right do we have to hold something over

another person? Remember that forgiveness is not a stamp of approval saying it is okay that a person hurt you. It is an act of the will, saying in your heart, "I release the right to hold this over you" or, "I will no longer hold this against you."

When we are generous with forgiveness, then bitterness, anger, and resentment flow away from us; but if we hold on to the offenses others have done toward us, we live in bondage and bitterness. Our lives become imprisoned by the pain we hold on to in our hearts. Release. The greatest gift you can give someone is the gift of love and forgiveness. Be generous.

Secret #4: Be a Positive Person

As we speak to countless women, we have found one common denominator women want in relationships: they want someone with whom they can laugh and enjoy life. So be an encourager, not a discourager. Laugh together. Plan fun things together.

Certainly there are times when we need to cry on each other's shoulders and share our challenges together, but we also need some good encouragement and laughter. As Proverbs says, "A cheerful look brings joy to the heart; good news makes for good health" (15:30).

The word *encourage* means to give strength. That's what we want to be about as friends. We want to strengthen each other as iron sharpens iron. Are you an encourager or a discourager? Do you build up your friends or do you spend most of the time whining and complaining, bringing them down? It's your choice, and you can choose today to be a positive friend.

What does a positive friend look like? She's not perfect, and she doesn't expect perfection in others. She enjoys her friends'

> All right believing in God is visibly reflected in right behavior towards men.
> —Geoffrey B. Wilson

company. She says uplifting things to her friends, cheering them on a regular basis. Her smile speaks a thousand words. It says, "I love you, my friend. I am choosing to overlook your faults and love you for who you are. I am choosing to enjoy life with you."

We have all had negative people in our lives who bring us down with their words or attitudes. Let's make sure that never describes us! Perhaps you're thinking, *You don't know me. I'm the negative, cup-half-empty sort of person.* We know that some people tend to think more negatively than others, but your thinking and your actions are still a choice. You can still choose to be a positive person with a spirit of encouragement and joy.

Remember that God's Spirit lives within those who follow Christ. His qualities are positive qualities. The Bible describes the fruit of God's Spirit as "love, joy, peace, patience, kindness, goodness, faithfulness, gentleness, and self-control" (Galatians 5:22–23). Those are certainly positive qualities. Ask God to help you live these qualities by the power of His Spirit at work in you.

Secret #5: Overlook Your Differences

We all have faults and little annoyances. We need to be big enough not to be petty. We need to look at the best in others, not the worst, because that is what we want others to do for us. We're so thankful for variety in life! Wouldn't life be boring if we were all exactly alike, acting and thinking the same way? Yet it is often those differences that tend to annoy us terribly.

We all were created with unique gifts, talents, and personalities. We handle situations and circumstances differently, and we don't all view life from the same angle. Instead of letting the differences separate us, we need to appreciate them, recognizing them as the unique way God made each one of us. (Quick side note: we are not talking about overlooking someone's habitual sin. That's a different story. We are talking about appreciating the different way people are made; we are not talking about bad or wrong choices people make. We need to gently help people caught in sin to get out of that sin.)

Take a quick moment to think of some of the little things that annoy you about others. Are you willing to shift your eyes off the annoyances and onto the good qualities about that person? Sometimes we need to stop and recognize that others annoy us because they simply react or handle life in a different way than we would choose. That's when we must appreciate God's variety in creation. May we never be so arrogant as to think that everyone should handle life and live life just as we would!

Aren't you glad that when you walk into a Baskin-Robbins ice-cream shop there are thirty-one flavors from which to choose? The trip to the ice-cream shop would be quite boring if we only had vanilla ice cream. Thank the Lord He made us with a variety of personalities and talents. Rejoice in them, enjoy them, but don't get bogged down in letting them make you angry and frustrated with others. Let's complement each other with our gifts instead of running the other way.

An honest man is the noblest work of God.
—Alexander Pope

Secret #6: Build on Your Common Interest

What brings you together with people in the first place? Reading, working out, cheering for a kid's soccer team, decorating? Build on it! Reflect on some of the common interests you have with the people around you and allow that to be a way to deepen the friendship. It may be as simple as liking the same restaurant, so set a date each month to meet at that restaurant for lunch. It could be that your kids are on the same sports team together. Grow your friendship as you sit on the bleachers watching them play.

Natural opportunities are all around us to build friendships in the course of our daily routines; we just need to recognize these opportunities and seize them. Think of some of the things you love to do and look for others who love to do the same. Perhaps you like to walk during your lunch break. Look and listen for someone else who enjoys walking and ask her to join you once a week. Build muscle and build a friendship in the process. A word of caution: if you are married, steer clear of building on a common interest with men. We play with fire when we work on building this type of connection outside of our marriage.

It's funny how easy it is to get the fifth and sixth secrets reversed. We tend to overlook our common interests with people and focus instead on our differences. This is especially true in marriages over the years. So take these two secrets and put them back in the right position, appreciating and overlooking differences while building on the common interests that brought you together in the first place.

> Friendship doubles joy and halves griefs.
> —Francis Bacon

72

Secret #7: Be Open, Honest, and Real

Don't wear masks. Nobody wants a perfect friend; we all want a real one. Sometimes we think people won't like us if they really know us. Not true! People tend to gravitate toward us more when we are vulnerable and open rather than when we seem picture-perfect and untouchable. Now certainly we don't want to flaunt our weaknesses and imperfections. There is a healthy balance, and it comes in being open, honest, and real with others.

Honesty truly is the basis for all relationships. People want friends they can
trust. Our words need to be truthful, not
full of flattery or deceit. Wise King Solomon
said, "A lying tongue hates its victims, and flat-
tery causes ruin" (Proverbs 26:28). Let's guard our tongues and allow only truth to come across our lips. Some things just don't need to be said at all, while other things need to be said in a gentle and loving way.

> Keep well thy tongue and keep thy friends.
> —Geoffrey Chaucer

As Polonius instructed his son in Shakespeare's *Hamlet*, "To thine own self be true." That's where genuine friendship begins and where masks fall off. Are we honest with ourselves? It's hard to really know ourselves. Even David, who was a man after God's own heart, asked the Lord, "Search me, O God, and know my heart; test me and know my thoughts. Point out anything in me that offends you, and lead me along the path of everlasting life" (Psalm 139:23–24). The Lord, who knows us through and through, can help us be honest with ourselves. Seek His help and ask Him to guide you to be the real and unique you that He created you to be.

73

Our Own Friendship

As we (Jane and Karol) look back at the journey of our friendship, we see the seven friendship principles at work in the developing of our own relationship. Although we are both Baylor grads, we didn't meet until several years out of college and well into our lives as moms. At the time we met, we each had written several books and were actively speaking to mothers' groups. Our common interests brought us together, and we began meeting periodically to share ideas and to encourage each other. A friendship was born as we opened up and shared and mourned our disappointments and rejoiced together over our successes. We recognized the value of being there for one

Five Fun Ideas to Do with Friends

- Grab coffee at the same meeting place and same time once a month (or week).

- Visit your favorite store, museum, or restaurant on a lunch hour.

- Work out together—lifting weights, walking, and talking form great bonds.

- Do charity work together on Saturday with kids (feeding the homeless, working for Special Olympics, or sorting donations at a women's shelter are wonderful opportunities to work together).

- Take the kids to a movie or athletic event or special show together.

another. Although our lives are busy, we were always able to put a regular lunchtime visit on the calendar.

Applying the Seven Secrets

Are you ready to be deliberate about the relationships in your life? Let's take a moment to examine how we can easily apply these seven principles to the relationships in our lives right now.

Write the names of several people in your life who are

Acquaintances:

_____

_____

Good Friends:

_____

_____

Soul Mates:

_____

_____

Now take each of the seven principles and decide how you can practically apply them to a person listed above to deepen the relationship.

1. This week I will take a genuine interest in _____

  by _____

2. Loyalty check: are there any people in my life right now with whom I am not being a loyal friend?

_____

3. Three ways I can give to my good friends this week are

_____

_____

_____

4. I will become more positive in my relationships by

_____

_____

5. I choose to overlook the annoyances and faults in others and instead see their finer qualities, such as

_____

_____

6. Common interests I have with some of the acquaintances in my life are

Person   Common Interest

_____   _____

_____   _____

_____   _____

7. I will be more open and real in the following areas:

_____

_____

8. Masks I tend to wear include

_____

_____

Happily Ever After

Maybe you feel, as we do, that marriage has two distinct phases: BC (before children) and AC (after children). The birth of a child alters your entire world, big time. If you're married, your life as a couple changes radically. Remembering to whisper sweet nothings into your chosen one's ear can slip your mind when faced with sleepless nights, work deadlines, mounds of diapers, and daily to-dos. The soul mate love you signed up for on your wedding day takes a backseat to the responsibilities parenthood brings. If we are not careful, our significant others can become insignificant strangers in no time flat.

Popular author and columnist Vicki Iovine explains it like this:

> Ironically, one of the biggest challenges to marriage is the fruit of the love fest, children. Mother Nature is so darn conni-ving, confusing us with a smokescreen of passion and Hallmark poetry to make us believe that having children with our beloved is the ultimate expression of our lifelong commitment. Until that first little cherub comes into your life you forge ahead with your reproductivity like a divine bulldozer, certain that fulfilling your biological imperative can only enhance your romance.[6]

Regaining equilibrium as a married couple after children change the scenery can be a hurdle. Career choices and financial implications brought on by new little lives cause us to pause for reevaluation. If we keep our relationship as a married couple strong, we provide a secure foundation for our children. This makes us better parents. But keeping that relationship strong comes down to plain hard work.

The good news is that God knows all about these challenges. Marriage is His invention, remember? In Genesis 2:24, we are told, "For this reason a man will leave his father and mother and be united to his wife, and they will become one flesh" (NIV). God set up this model for a lifetime, committed relationship between a man and a woman to provide a solid basis for the family. God's design is perfect, but the day-to-day humdrum of life's circumstances often can cause the intended lifetime commitment to lose its pizazz. Making pizazz a priority helps the marriage relationship make it over the long haul.

Eight Ways to Say "I Love You" to the Man in Your Life

- Send an "I love you" card to his office or try an e-card for a pleasant surprise in the middle of a hectic day.

- Read *The Language of Love* by Gary Smalley and John Trent. Learn how to communicate in word pictures so your husband can understand your point of view.

- Place a small box of chocolates in his briefcase (but not on a hot day!).

- Fill his car with gas when he would least expect it and most need it.

- Have an art time with your kids and ask them to create a picture for Daddy's office. Roll up the picture and tie it with a ribbon.

- Purchase a subscription to his favorite magazine or business journal.

- Bake his favorite dessert for him, or better yet, order it from his favorite restaurant and have it couriered to his office.

- Give him an evening of complete relaxation. Take the kids somewhere and give him the remote or schedule a massage, manicure, or golf game.

Pizazz Prescription

Anne Morrow Lindbergh said, "Good communication is as stimulating as black coffee, and just as hard to go to sleep after." Unresolved marital issues can cause communication between spouses to become less than stimulating. This is where forgiveness needs to present itself front and center. We all know that in times of conflict it is easy to pull down that window-shade list of how we might have been wronged over the years, thus adding to the strife. But if we choose to forgive and focus on why we married our spouse in the first place, perhaps our marital communication can take on that black-coffee effect.

Beverly Sills says, "There are no shortcuts to anyplace worth going." This statement sums up our journey in marriage. There are no shortcuts to commitment. Want to put the punch back in your marital partnership? Start here. Stop just a moment and reflect on these questions:

Why did you fall in love with your husband?

_____

_____

What qualities do you admire in your husband?

_____

_____

What differences did you find endearing during the dating game?

_____

_____

Which of those quirks drive you crazy now?

_____

_____

Stepping back and taking a good, long look at where your marriage began and why you began it can be just the caffeine boost you and your spouse need as you juggle marriage, children, work, and life.

We well know that pizazz does not stop with taking a little inventory—it starts with deliberate action. From Karol's book *The Power of a Positive Wife*, we share a few ideas for being a creative lover and reconnecting in a romantic way.

Build the interest and anticipation for a late-night delight with your hubby by giving him a few playful hints throughout the day. Yes, you can and should flirt with your husband! Here are some fun ideas to try:

- *Write him a short, sexy note* letting him know your hopes and intentions for later: "Can't wait for you to get home tonight, big boy." "Let's get hot and heavy tonight, handsome." "Let's have some fun after the kids go to bed tonight." Put the note where only he will see it at home, or sneak it into his briefcase or pocket. Warning: Do be careful that the note doesn't get into the wrong hands! I know a woman who wrote a sexy note to her husband on the back of what she thought was one of her child's old school papers. It was actually a homework assignment that had to be turned in the next day. The child came home from school with a note from the teacher saying, "I thought you might want this note back—and next time be careful where you write a note to your husband!"

- *Touch your husband or rub his back.* Get to know how he likes to be touched, and look for the right timing. A soft, sexy, flirtatious touch can build the mood and give the nonverbal cue that you are looking forward to later.

- *Write a note on your bathroom mirror using a dry-erase marker.* Tell him you are looking forward to a "hot and steamy" time tonight. Add a lipstick impression of your lips. (Yes, kiss the mirror after you have applied an abundance of lipstick!)

- *Call him at the office* and, using a soft, sexy voice, tell him you are looking forward to him coming home from work. Make sure he is not on a speakerphone!

- *Cuddle with him while you are still in bed* in the morning. Let him know your hopeful intentions for that evening. Tell him you will be looking forward to your special time together all through the day.

- *Prepare a romantic candlelight dinner.* (If you have kids, send them to Grandma's house or arrange for them to spend the evening with friends.) The room should be dimly lit, with romantic music playing in the background. Look into his eyes, listen to him, and don't talk about the cares of the day or the children's activities. Smile and enjoy each other's company.[7]

Keep Your Heart in the Right Place

An old saying reminds us, "He who seeks the perfect friend remains without one." If you are searching for Ms. Wonderful Friend or a friend who will meet all your expectations or even a perfect husband, stop searching. There is only one who fits the title of Wonderful. There is only one perfect friend, and that is Christ Himself. He is the only one who can fulfill all of our needs. He loves us completely and unconditionally. He forgives us, and He is always with us. He gave us His very life.

No one else can completely love us as He can. When we put our hope in people, they will disappoint us every time. Our hope must be in the Lord and His unfailing love and faithfulness. The apostle Paul reminded the early Christians that Christ is our "all in all" (Ephesians 1:23 NKJV). Is Christ your all in all, or are you seeking fulfillment and satisfaction in your husband or your kids or your job? When we place our love and focus on Christ first, our relationships fall into proper perspective. When we are centered on people or things, our balance gets off center, and we become needy, dependent, and easily frustrated and annoyed.

Giving is truly healing.
—Charles H. Spurgeon

So the real secret to lasting and meaningful relationships is to keep our hearts in the right place. May each of us place our heart's desires in Christ's loving arms. Let's look to Him for our true and pure love. As we relish His love, we soon begin to see that we reflect His love in the way we love others. When we know how deeply and completely we are loved, we will discover that it is so much easier to love others. Let's rest in the security of knowing we are completely loved by Him.

How Well Do You Relate to Men?

Respond to this statement: "I find myself intimidated by men in positions of authority."

    a. I avoid situations where this may be true.

    b. This happens occasionally.

    c. This is no truer of men than of women.

    d. This is usually true.

How would you characterize your childhood relationship with your father?

    a. Nonexistent

    b. Distant

    c. Comfortable

    d. Unhealthy

If you and your guy have opposing views, do you

    a. Rarely voice your preferences?

    b. Give in rather than create tension?

    c. Discuss areas of disagreement?

    d. Feel insecure or threatened?

Little boys are

    a. More difficult than little girls.

    b. More independent than little girls.

    c. More energetic than little girls.

    d. More aggressive than little girls.

Little girls are

a. *More cautious than little boys.*

b. *More delicate than little boys.*

c. *More sensitive than little boys.*

d. *More emotional than little boys.*

Which of the following best describes you?

a. *I am not very confident.*

b. *I have some areas of insecurity.*

c. *I am basically comfortable with myself.*

d. *I sometimes wish I were someone else.*

Which of these words would you use to describe yourself?

a. *Unreadable*

b. *Aloof*

c. *Different*

d. *Dynamic*

Which of these sounds more appealing?

a. *Enjoying a good movie at a theater with your guy*

b. *A double date with close friends*

c. *Dinner with your guy at a quiet restaurant*

d. *An evening at the carnival, complete with cotton candy*

Do conversations with men:

a. *Happen rarely?*

b. *Make you uncomfortable?*

c. *Give you an interesting perspective on various subjects?*

d. *Make you nervous?*

85

Do you find it difficult to trust men?

a. *Often*

b. *Sometimes*

c. *Occasionally*

d. *Always*

Scoring:

If you chose *a* most often, men are basically beyond your understanding. They think and act in ways that are alien to you, and you don't trust what you can't understand. You may have found it difficult to find or maintain a meaningful relationship.

If you chose *b* most often, you tend to see men as insensitive and detached. In any relationship with a man, you feel a need to prove your value and rarely consider you have succeeded. You tend to be a bit too dependent on and possessive with that one special guy.

If you chose *c* most often, you have a healthy view of male/female relationships. You probably find it fairly easy to relate to men and consider them intriguing. Once you have found your special guy, you have no problem with commitment, and he will most likely become your best friend.

If you chose *d* most often, you tend to feel threatened by men and may have found yourself in some unhealthy relationships. You tend to consider men overwhelming and may feel somewhat hostile toward them. You want nothing more than a stable, loving relationship but find it difficult to attain.[8]

The Relationship Factor at a Glance

- To have good friends, we must be a good friend.

- Look for ways to add pizazz to your marital partnership.

- In order to experience genuine friendships, we must make love a priority.

- Developing and sustaining strong friendships doesn't take more time; it takes intention.

The Seven Secrets of Meaningful Relationships

- Take a genuine interest in other people.

- Be loyal.

- Be a giver, not a taker.

- Be a positive person.

- Overlook your differences.

- Build on your common interest.

- Be open, honest, and real.

The real secret to lasting and meaningful relationships is to keep our hearts in the right place—focused on Jesus Christ.

meditations
for the frazzled soul

We have heard of your faith in Christ Jesus and of the love you have for all the saints.

COLOSSIANS 1:4 NIV

He who refreshes others will himself be refreshed.

PROVERBS 11:25 NIV

Give, and it will be given to you. A good measure, pressed down, shaken together and running over, will be poured into your lap.

LUKE 6:38 NIV

Two are better than one, because they have a good return for their work.

ECCLESIASTES 4:9 NIV

A friend is always loyal, and a brother is born to help in time of need.

PROVERBS 17:17

Loyalty makes a person attractive.

PROVERBS 19:22

The most important piece of clothing you must wear is love. Love is what binds us all together in perfect harmony.

COLOSSIANS 3:14

"Oh, that? I thought I told you. 'Dateline NBC' is going to feature us in a segment titled 'Working Couples: Who Does the Brunt of the Housework?'"

chapter 4

The Business Factor
Equipping Yourself for Success

Successful people make important decisions
early in their life, then they spend the rest of their life
managing those decisions.

—JOHN MAXWELL

Katie owns a successful personal training and fitness business in
North Dallas. As the sole proprietor of her business and a single
mom, her clients and her kids depend on her each day. On a
delightful afternoon not too long ago, Katie picked up her youngest
daughter, Alexa, from preschool, only to hear her announce that
she had a bead stuck in her ear. Yes, you read that right: she had
stuck a bead in her ear (apparently she was bored during nap time).
Katie tried to get the bead out of Alexa's ear, but she couldn't do it
and ended up taking Alexa to the doctor. Unfortunately, the bead
was so deeply imbedded that it could only be removed by putting
Alexa to sleep. Costs of day surgery, missed work, and disappointed
clients all raced through Katie's mind as she began making the fourteen phone calls to reschedule her clients for the next day.

Success in business? What about simple survival? Is it possible for a mother to maintain success in both business and home
life, especially when the unexpected happens and the two worlds
collide? A mom in the workplace has different challenges than

others in the workplace, but through flexibility and adaptation she can reach her goals in her business and in family life. In this chapter we want to equip you with innovative and practical tools for success designed specifically for the needs of moms.

Our discovery process began several years ago as the professional challenges in our own lives led us to a fact-finding mission. We accepted an invitation from a major corporation in Dallas to investigate the felt needs common to most working mothers. As we sat in the boardroom filled with working moms and listened to their struggles and cries for help, it became quite evident that each of the women deeply desired to do her best and be her best in both her work life and her home life. These women acknowledged their challenges and exposed their frustration in trying to juggle their responsibilities as corporate women. They disclosed a long list of issues that seemed to throw them off balance and shared suggestions for sanity solutions. With one voice, they pleaded for more ways to win the seemingly impossible synchronized work/home performance.

Forget a corporate coach or a better day planner. These women asked for daily doables to equip themselves for success. As a result of this corporate focus group, we have created a five-step plan to help equip moms in any line of work (or even volunteer responsibility) to experience success in achieving their goals. Perhaps "success" is not what you are after. Maybe it's just a job to you. You do it and go home. If that describes you, then allow this chapter to give you a glimmer of joy, fulfillment, and excitement about your job, no matter how mundane it may seem. We hope that after reading this chapter you will see your work not just as a job, but as a way to honor God with your time.

Define Success

Success is not the same for everyone. For Sandra, success may be finishing the pile that looms on her desk before she leaves for home. Success to Debi may be bringing three new clients to her advertising firm. Patti sees success as raising seventy-five thousand dollars for the local private school through the auction she is chairing. Joellen defines success as seeing one of her patients finally take that first step after months of physical therapy and rehabilitation.

Define *success* for you. If we don't define it, success remains a nebulous, unachievable idea. When we define success, we begin to see it clearly, work toward it, and recognize when we get close to achieving it. It is also important to realize that there are short-term successes that we can experience and long-term goals that we can work toward.

Focusing on what we are trying to achieve helps us forge ahead and weather some of the unplanned challenges and responsibilities that pop into our lives. Let's keep our eyes on our goal and not on our immediate circumstances. John R. Noe said, "Losers always concentrate on activities, but high achievers concentrate on planning and making every moment count in their efforts to reach progressively higher intermediate goals."[1]

The writer of Hebrews tells us we are to keep our eyes ultimately on our eternal goal, our purpose for life: "Let us run with endurance the race that God has set

> If you go to work on your goals, your goals will go to work on you. If you go to work on your plan, your plan will go to work on you. Whatever good things we build end up building us.
> —Jim Rohn

before us. We do this by keeping our eyes on Jesus, on whom our faith depends from start to finish. He was willing to die a shameful death on the cross because of the joy he knew would be his afterward" (Hebrews 12:1–2). Through the pain, Jesus kept His eyes on the bigger picture of what He was to accomplish on the cross. We too must keep our eyes on the bigger picture through the daily challenges we face.

As you fill in the blanks below, be realistic in what you feel you can accomplish in God's timing and strength. Stretch yourself, yes, but don't overwhelm yourself by setting too lofty of a goal. Prayerfully fill in the following blanks:

Yearly Business Success Goal

This year at work, I want to accomplish

_____

Three-Year Business Success Goal

Within the next three years, I would like to accomplish

_____

Five-Year Business Success Goal

Five years from now, I plan to

_____

Your goals may change throughout the years due to family situations or unexpected circumstances. Remain flexible and set new goals if you need to. The point is to have a business success goal toward which you are working and one that will keep your focus on the bigger picture and not the immediate challenges. Ultimately and always we want to keep our eyes on the Lord and His plan and purpose for our lives. Where He guides us, He will provide for us.

Equip for Success

What does it take to be equipped to reach our goals? Using the acronym EQUIP, we created a simple, five-step formula for staying on track toward your business success goals: *education, quest, understanding, integrity,* and *perseverance.* These five letters will become your cue cards or a checks-and-balances system for running the race.

In 1 Corinthians 9:24–25, Paul says, "Do you not know that in a race all the runners run, but only one gets the prize? Run in such a way as to get the prize. Everyone who competes in the games goes into strict training. They do it to get a crown that will not last; but we do it to get a crown that will last forever" (NIV). Without a doubt, we are running a race; let's just make sure it is not a rat race. Our race can be a victorious journey as we run steady and strong with our eyes on the goal and purpose that God has for our lives.

Education

Educate yourself as much as possible about your business. What makes it work? Who are the most successful people within your line of work? What can you learn from them? Perhaps you are saying, "I barely have time to complete my project list at work. Exactly when am I supposed to educate myself?" We do not mean that you have to read stacks and stacks of books; however, if a new, popular one surfaces, a review of the contents page might prove insightful. Try these quick tips for business brain food.

- Find an expert in your business and offer to buy him or her a quick lunch, identifying your fact-finding intentions.

- Join online e-newsletters for quick tips on current topics.

- Attend associational workshops and conventions.

- Visit business-related web sites.

- Create a buddy system by asking one colleague to be responsible for certain business trends while you research other aspects, then meet and compare notes.

Charles "Tremendous" Jones was right when he said, "There are essentially two things that will make you wiser, the books you read and the people you meet."[2] People + reading = quality education. Let's educate ourselves along the pathway to business success in order to be the best we can be.

Quest

What do we mean by quest? The word *quest* means a search, pursuit, or hunt. In medieval times, a quest was a journey in search of adventure, an expedition of heroic proportions. The life of a working mom can certainly be described as heroic at times, don't you agree?

Our quest as working moms is to see the purpose in the work

God has given us and to do our work to the best of our ability. The apostle Paul told the early Christians, "Work hard and cheerfully at whatever you do, as though you were working for the Lord rather than for people" (Colossians 3:23). What a wonderful charge for us all! Our quest begins as we realize that our ultimate employer is the Lord Himself. We serve Him, we answer to Him, and we represent Him in what we do in this world. When we recognize our Boss, we set our standards and work ethic at a higher level. Our quest is to please Him and not simply to earn more money or please people.

To do our best in work, we must enjoy our work. We work more than we play, so at the very least, liking what we do is essential to making a good life. What about you: are you enjoying your work? If you can't change jobs, choose to look at your present job in a different light. You will begin to see your work with a fresh new perspective and vigor. When we see our job as an opportunity to serve God and love people, it gives us a whole new outlook.

Here are four quest points:

- View your job as a service to God.

- Ask God to give you the strength and direction you need to do your best.

- Take responsibility for your actions.

- Be innovative and look for new ways to do your best.

How can God use you and your gifts and talents in the workplace? What does He want to do through you? No job is mundane when we see it as service to our Lord.

97

Viewing our best from an eternal perspective invites God into your work. When we keep our eyes on God's purpose and perspective, we find the verse in Isaiah written just for us: "Those who hope in the LORD will renew their strength. They will soar on wings like eagles; they will run and not grow weary, they will walk and not be faint" (Isaiah 40:31 NIV). Our quest is to be women who soar like eagles. Let us take flight, looking toward God's finish line, and do our very best at our jobs.

Understanding

The prayer of St. Francis of Assisi says, "Lord, grant that I may not so much seek to be understood as to understand." Have you ever wished that others would take a few minutes and try, really try, to understand you or perhaps your innovative ideas? Knowing and feeling we have been heard validates us as human beings. When we take time to hear, really hear, the people closest to us, we add significance to their ideas, thus making them feel valued.

Whom do we need to understand? Our employer, our co-workers, our office staff, our husband, our kids, our friends—and the list goes on. But how in the world can we be universally understanding of others? Here are several keys to help you better understand the people in your life:

- *Listen with your heart, mind, and soul.* Maintain eye contact and make sure your thoughts are focused on the person you are with at the time.

- *Repeat what you think you have heard.* Sometimes we assume the best or the worst, and we don't really hear the facts. Think about what you have heard, repeat what they said, and together, make a plan.

- *Review history.* Has anything ever happened like this before? If so, what did you learn from it? If not, what can you do now to better the circumstance?

- *Come from an open and learning perspective*, not an "I-know-it-all" perspective.

Real understanding is a process, not a slam dunk. As we journey down our road to success, our understanding of others will lead us along. We especially want to understand what is expected of us at work and what our families expect of us at home. In fact, before taking on any new responsibilities (whether at work, at home, or as a volunteer), it is important to ask questions and gain a full understanding of what is expected of us. Typically it is safe to assume that the responsibilities and time commitment will turn out to be greater than what you are first told.

When we must miss work due to a child's illness or a special family event, we need to understand our employer's perspective. How will this affect him or her? What burden does this put on your coworkers? What can you do to make your absence from work easier for everyone involved? We also want to have an understanding of our families. If you miss your daughter's track meet, how important is that to her? Will

> If there is any one secret of success, it lies in the ability to get the other person's point of view and see things from that person's angle as well as from your own.
> —Henry Ford

your husband be bothered if you don't attend the luncheon with him? Understanding our family's individual needs can help us sort through what is necessary and what only seems necessary.

Integrity

Honesty—don't leave home without it. We are ambassadors for Christ (see 2 Corinthians 5:20), and honesty is a key ingredient in our life description. When it comes to our work, there is one area we cannot compromise, and that is the area of integrity. In a world of blurred standards and situational ethics, we must have the courage to stand on truth, which means we may sometimes be standing alone.

How does integrity play out in work? Being honest on the timecard, owning up to responsibility, not sharing stories about a coworker behind her back, showing up on time, and not leaving early. Yes, integrity plays a part moment by moment in our work.

Webster's Dictionary defines *integrity* as "an unimpaired condition; the quality or state of being complete or undivided."³ The bottom line is that *integrity* is a fancy term for honesty in the trenches of everyday life. Integrity is knowing and living your values. Do you approach your business with integrity? Every day we must purpose to use integrity as the foundation of our business platform.

How do we approach our work with integrity? Here are four steps to living honestly.

- *Know what you believe* and create a values statement.

- *Do a self-check.* What is lurking within your life? Honesty begins with being honest with yourself.

- *Find an accountability partner.* As you identify areas of personal temptation, seek a friend with whom you can be accountable.

- *Study the Bible* as the foundation for your lifestyle and values.

Perseverance

Henry Longfellow said, "Perseverance is a great element of success. If you only knock long enough and loud enough at the gate you are sure to wake up somebody."[4] Do you ever feel as though you have been knocking forever, knuckles bruised and patience wearing thin? Hang in there, and keep knocking; opportunity is beginning to wake. Are you discouraged because the challenges of life seem overwhelming? Persevere, for this too shall pass.

We love the story of the highschool basketball coach who tried to motivate his team and encourage them to persevere through a challenging and difficult season. At one midseason pep talk, he made a short but effective speech. "Did Shaquille O'Neal ever quit?" he asked. The team replied in unison, "No!" The coach continued, "What about the Wright Brothers; did they ever give up?" "No!" came the reply. "What about Peyton Manning; did he ever throw in the towel?" A resounding "No!" filled the locker room. "And what about Elmer McAllister; did he quit?"

After an awkward silence, one brave student asked, "Who's Elmer McAllister?" "Who is Elmer McAllister, you ask? We have never heard of him," the coach snapped back. "Do you know why we have never heard of him? Because he quit, that's why!"

> The three great essentials to achieve anything worthwhile are, first, hard work; second, stick-to-itiveness; third, common sense.
> —Thomas Edison

Perseverance—a courageous strength to hang in there when the going gets tough. We need perseverance in our work, in our relationships, and in our circumstances. The early Christians learned what perseverance looked like as they faced persecution for their faith. The writer of Hebrews encouraged these early Christians, who were in the midst of many trials, with these words: "Patient endurance is what you need now, so you will continue to do God's will. Then you will receive all that he has promised" (Hebrews 10:36). May we each have patient endurance through the tough times and around the difficult people life brings.

Here are some tips to keep in mind as you persist and persevere through your life's circumstances.

- *Pray.* Ask God to help you have the courage, strength, and wisdom to persevere.

- *Determine if it is worth persevering.* Sometimes it is better to move on to a new job or situation. If you have made a commitment, as much as possible stay with it, but if there is flexibility, consider the cost.

- *Seek wise counsel,* perhaps from someone who understands your situation or who has walked in your shoes.

- *Acquire an encourager.* Ask a friend to stand with you and encourage you through the tough times.

In our profession, we (Jane and Karol) have seen countless potential writers and authors fall by the wayside. Why? Lack of persistence. In order to be a writer, you must submit your work to editors; and the first rule of the trade is "Expect rejection." Even the greatest writers of all times received rejection letters. Tolstoy was rejected seventeen times before a publisher finally agreed to publish *War and Peace*. Rejection doesn't feel good, and most of us don't enjoy it; but persistent writers end up being published writers.

Are you feeling discouraged in your business? Don't give up until you have exhausted all possibilities. Stick with it, persist, learn from your mistakes, seek wise counsel, and if it is meant to be, the doors of opportunity will eventually open.

Clear Your Focus

Focus is difficult for both of us. In fact, we are card-carrying members of Hummingbird Heads Anonymous. This is an organization for ladies who flit from one task to another. Actually, to call this an "organization" is totally incorrect; it should be referred to as a "non-organization." To be a full-fledged member of HHA requires disorganization as a prime qualification.

Stellar intentions are another qualifying attribute for HHA membership. Sound familiar? In our defense, we are a fun group with lots of laughs, sensational snacks, and delightful fellowship. We suffer from a sort of "birds-of-a-feather-flock-together" syndrome.

> People with clear, written goals accomplish far more in a shorter period of time than people without them could ever imagine.
> —Brian Tracy

Now, this is not making light of those with medical conditions that impair their focus; this is telling the truth about those multitaskers who need a good shot in the arm with a focus vaccine.

How do you know if you qualify for Hummingbird Heads Anonymous? Here are the qualifications for membership:

1. You find yourself disorganized despite tremendous intentions.

2. You are pile challenged.

3. Your car has last week's Happy Meal in the backseat. Okay, let's be honest. It probably has last year's Happy Meal fries lodged under the backseat.

4. On your way to the store you forget what you need to buy.

5. You own more than five books on the topic of organization.

6. Your hair stands on end when around the overtly organized.

7. You pay late fees for library books and videotapes on a regular basis.

8. You can be a lot of fun.

9. You enjoy gooey snacks rich in fat, especially halved with other HHA members.

10. Right this moment you do not know where your car keys are.

If you can answer yes to at least seven of these items, then welcome to the flock, sister. Beware of the intense, left-brain, linear thinkers who would find our group appalling; in fact, they could probably *fix* us if given the chance. Whether you are a Hummingbird Head or a ducks-in-a-row type of person, we can never underestimate the benefits of staying focused in our work.

Perhaps you have heard the statement, "Wherever you are, be there." When at work, we need to be fully engaged in work, but when we take off the work hat and put on the mother and wife hat, we need to be fully engaged in family. Easier said than done, right? How can we wear our hats well? Here are a few hat-switching tips.

Decide

Every day we must take decisive action to focus on the tasks of the day. Decide to focus on the present and to plan for the future. It is important that we make a conscious decision to disengage from work each day before we reach home. Do what absolutely needs to be finished before you leave work, and then choose a time of disengagement or transition each day. If you have a drive or commute home, this can be your time of transition. If you work at home, set aside a short period of time before the kids get home from school or up from their naps.

Determine

During this time of transition, determine what needs to be done during the next workday. Make lists to plan the next day so that you can take your plans out of your brain and put them onto paper. Once something is written down, determine that you will not worry or think about it until you have time to deal with it the next day. Determine how you will brighten your children's day as you journey home. It may be a word of encouragement, a listening ear, a hug, or a smile, but choose something you will do deliberately.

Ways to be Effective
When Working at Home

- Set deadlines that have negative consequences if you miss them.

- Have a buddy, colleague, coach, or staff member who keeps you focused.

- If you don't love what you do, change it so that you do.

- Develop a routine—or don't.

- Train your family members what work time means.

- Make your home office absolutely perfect.

- Keep your beverages and snacks close at hand.

- Set daily goals.

- Get off to a great start for the day.

- Have something interesting to work on for the next day.

(Source: Thomas J. Leonard, *Working Wisdom: Lists for Improving Your Business* (Austin, Tex.: Bard Press, 1997), 113.)

Deal, Delegate, but Always Delete

If there are projects or worries hanging over your head as you transition from work to home or from home to work, then you have a choice to deal with them, delegate them, or delete them from your mind for the present. If at all possible before you make the transition, you need to deal with the situation to the best of your ability, delegate it to some-one else, or delegate it to another day. Whichever way you choose to handle the situation, the bottom line is that you must delete it from your mind and not worry or dwell on it when you are not at work (or not at home, as the case may be).

> How am I going to live today in order to create the tomorrow I'm committed to?
> —Anthony Robbins

Live in the present. Be where you are. When at work, be at work; when at home, be at home. Keeping your focus seems like a simple strategy, yet it is paramount to your business success.

Assess Your Business Strengths and Weaknesses

Gwen Moran, the founder of BoostYourBiz.com, shares this thought on her web site: "While it may seem a bit callous to define you as a product—after all, women are each unique individuals—adopting some of the most basic principles of marketing can help you focus on landing the opportunities that are right for you. That could mean climbing the corporate ladder or launching your own business."[5]

So how does a marketing professional create a plan? Here is a checklist:

- Review and critique what is being marketed. (What are your abilities?)

- Know where you want to go to get the word out. (What is your career goal?)

- Create a three-minute personal sales pitch. (Do you have an up-to-date résumé?)

- Buff up your outward image. (Need a new do or clothing style?)

- Go tell it on the mountain. (Help others catch your vision.)

- Get confident and sell yourself. (Be confident in what you have to offer.)

Focus on what you do well. Playing on your strengths is manipulation of the best kind. We all have talents we like; we all have weaknesses we don't like. In the working world, it pays to take advantage of the fact that, without a doubt, there is something you do very well. Why not concentrate on your strong points and sidestep those personal drawbacks you'd like to forget about? We all know what it feels like to be "in the zone" or working at our highest level in our most enjoyable task.

Each of us can benefit from a SWOT analysis—an assessment of your business *strengths, weaknesses, opportunities,* and *threats.* Think candidly about the following questions. You may want to ask a close friend or business associate to help you answer these truthfully.

What are your business strengths?

_____

_____

What are some of those weaknesses you don't want to think about?

_____

_____

What are your business opportunities?

_____

_____

What circumstances pose a threat to your business?

_____

_____

Cartoonist Randy Glasbergen created a poignant piece in which a dejected character is panhandling with a sign that reads "Accidentally listened to my motivation tapes backwards and became a failure. Please help."[6] Sometimes we just need to re-organize, refocus, and review where we are in order to go in the right direction.

Now that you have self-assessed, you are prepared to self-address. First, take at least a few minutes to celebrate what is working. Congratulations. Remember, the road to confidence is paved with weekly victories, so learn to applaud them. Concentrate first on what is right, and then move to improve the concerns that need your attention. What do you do with ease that other people find difficult? We are talking about your natural, God-given talents (not just business strengths) that may be transferable to your financial bottom line. It is our charge to recognize our talents and use them for the glory of God.

Take a minute and list two of your talents.

_____

_____

"My degree and work experience are in computers," you may say, "but my talent is in art. It would be totally irresponsible to change my direction and focus on my natural ability. I can't afford that." Maybe so, for this season, but what about taking baby steps toward what you do best and see what happens? The best-selling book *The Power of Focus* shares this advice: "When you focus most of your time and energy doing the things you are truly brilliant at, you eventually reap big rewards. This is a fundamental truth. And it's critical to your future success."[7]

Start Networking with Others

Networking can often be taken as a negative, self-serving, self-promoting concept—a sort of "what's-in-it-for-me" mentality. In reality, networking approached through the concept of the golden rule ("Do unto others as you would have them do unto you") suddenly becomes a gift from God for you and for those you know. "Networking is not about selling yourself, but helping others. It's about building mutually beneficial relationships," says Kathleen Barton, author of *Connecting with Success: How to Build a Mentoring*

Network to Fast-Forward Your Career. "If your focus is on building relationships and being a resource to others, then people will value you. They will want to help you reach your goals as well."[8]

We need each other. God didn't create us to be self-sufficient islands; He created us as connectors. Vance Havner once said, "Christians, like snowflakes, are frail, but when they stick together they can stop traffic."[9] What is your plan for stopping traffic through working together and networking with other people?

We all need to know and practice networking. Soon you'll develop a strategy that works best for you. Here are some questions to get you thinking:

- What is your current network of friends and business associates?

- Do you frequently offer to assist others in developing their network?

- What type of network do you want to develop?

- Who are three people you might help? Repeat this process each week.

Effective networking involves building relationships. Build-ing relationships involves listening with your heart. Listening with your heart shows and establishes genuine interest. Networking is not about the results, although that can be a bonus; it is about the relationships. Our goal is to build a network with *real* relation-ships. A growing leader needs a relational network that includes mentors, peers, and people whom he or she can mentor.

There is a common thread among leaders who finish well. Without exception, successful leaders have a significant network of people who inspired them and held them accountable. As growing leaders, a network of strong relationships helps to ensure our personal development and a healthy perspective on our life and mission. The key is: don't collect people, relate to them.

Let's face it: we all like to be appreciated. Mark Twain once said, "I can live two months on a good compliment."[10] We agree. Nothing can put the spring back in your step like knowing without a doubt that someone took notice of your efforts and took time to say so. In Dottie Gandy's book *30 Days to a Happy Employee*, she explains:

> Business surveys tell us that when we feel sufficiently valued for our contributions, we feel better and perform better. This is certainly true for women. Working moms are often fulfilling several careers simultaneously. It's important for us to know that we are appreciated for our efforts. One of the ways to help insure that we get regular and intentional acknowledgment is to give it to those around us. Not only can this be a key to our success, it can be a key to our sanity.[11]

We can sum up the transforming truths of this chapter in three words: *equip, focus,* and *network.* Equip yourselves to be the best you can be at work. Focus on your strengths, abilities, and talents, not on your weaknesses. Enjoy the blessing of being around others in your field.

Most important, we want to encourage you to love your life by enjoying your work and loving your family.

How Assertive Are You?

When involved in a project with a group of people,

    a. I prefer to be in a leadership role.

    b. I prefer to be assigned a specific task.

    c. I enjoy the interaction and differing ideas.

The best work usually comes from

    a. A person with knowledge and vision.

    b. A well-developed plan.

    c. The merging of creative minds.

When making an important decision,

    a. I trust my insight and reasoning.

    b. I weigh all the options carefully and discuss the matter with a close friend.

    c. I seek the opinions of those I trust.

Others probably see me as

    a. Capable and resourceful.

    b. Dependable and cooperative.

    c. Open and receptive.

If I make a mistake,

    a. I determine not to repeat it.

    b. I learn from it and go on.

    c. I am the first to admit it.

When in charge,
    a. I make sure I have all the facts.
    b. I consider all decisions carefully and appreciate wise advice.
    c. I make use of all resources at hand.

I am most easily offended by
    a. Insults.
    b. False accusations.
    c. Insensitivity.

I strive to
    a. Develop.
    b. Become.
    c. Learn.

I dislike
    a. Failure.
    b. Chaos.
    c. Conflict.

I like being in the position to
    a. Follow through on ideas.
    b. Gain a new perspective.
    c. Bring harmony to discord.

Scoring:

a = 3 points

b = 2 points

c = 1 point

Add your total points to arrive at your score. If you scored:

1–16: You may be too easily swayed by the opinions and view-points of others. It is good to be open to new perspectives, but at some point you need to take a stand for what you believe. Scripture reveals truth. If you base your decisions on that truth, you can stand with courage and conviction.

17–22: You have a good, basic understanding of the value of cooperation. A wise person recognizes her own strengths and limitations and is willing to learn from others. The analogy found in 1 Corinthians 12:12–27 gives us a biblical view of interaction and purpose. You intuitively possess this insight. It is a gift to those around you.

23–30: Confidence is not a character flaw, but taken too far it can appear as arrogance. It is not weakness to admit limitation. Overt assertiveness can point to egotism and feelings of superiority. It can also be a cover for insecurity. Regardless of its cause, it is an attitude contrary to productivity and destructive to relationships and self-improvement. As we are told in Proverbs 12:15, "Fools think they are doing right, but the wise listen to advice" (NCV).

(Source: Laurie Whaley and Beverly Riggs, eds., *Becoming*, NCV Bible [Nashville: Thomas Nelson, 2004], 257.)

The Business Factor at a Glance

- If we don't define *success*, it remains a nebulous, unachievable idea.

- Keep your focus on the bigger picture: your life goals and your eternal perspective.

- Flexibility is a key component when planning goals.

- Never underestimate the benefits of staying focused.

- Review your SWOT analysis. Know your strengths, weaknesses, opportunities, and threats.

- Discern your talents, decide how to use them, and delegate the tasks outside your best ability when possible.

- Effective networking involves building relationships.

- Equip, focus, and network to be successful at work.

EQUIP for Success

- Education—Learn as much as possible about your business.

- Quest—Strive to please God and not simply to earn more money or please people.

- Understanding—Take time to really hear the people closest to you.

- Integrity—Alexander Pope said, "An honest man's the noblest work of God."

- Perseverance—Patient endurance is a great element of success.

meditations
for the frazzled soul

Give her the reward she has earned, and let her works bring her praise at the city gate.

PROVERBS 31:31 NIV

Whatever you do, work at it with all your heart, as working for the Lord, not for men.

COLOSSIANS 3:23 NIV

For we are God's workmanship, created in Christ Jesus to do good works, which God prepared in advance for us to do.

EPHESIANS 2:10 NIV

The man who plants and the man who waters have one purpose, and each will be rewarded according to his own labor. For we are God's fellow workers; you are God's field, God's building.

1 CORINTHIANS 3:8–9 NIV

chapter 5

The Fun Factor

Celebrating the Joys of Life

Keep looking for the boomerang surprise in your life.
Listen for the whirring sound that means it may be
getting close. Always stay connected to people and seek
out things that bring you joy. Dream with abandon.

—BARBARA JOHNSON

All work and no play makes a woman's life quite dull, don't you think? How strong is the fun factor in your life? You may be saying, "Fun? What in the world is that?" Do you view fun and play as something you did "once upon a time"? In most of our lives, fun typically comes at the very bottom of a long list of things to do. This chapter is all about reintroducing you to fun and reminding you of the benefits of fun in your life.

Let's think of fun as a recess from the responsibilities of life. It can include hobbies, relaxation, personal time, and stress reduction. Wholehearted fun is surrounded with humor, amusement, and laughter, and it could mean the difference between serious burnout and living life to its fullest.

"Humor is one of God's most marvelous gifts. . . . Humor reveals the roses and hides the thorns. Humor makes our heavy burdens light and smoothes the rough spots in our pathways," says comedian Sam J. Ervin.[1] No wonder the Bible tells us, "A cheerful heart is good medicine, but a broken spirit saps a person's strength" (Proverbs 17:22). We all need a good dose of cheer and fun in our life as a sort of shock absorber from the cares and worries of this world.

What tends to foil our fun or rain on our parade? Often the culprit can be a packed schedule, an overly serious attitude, or the burdens of business. Perhaps you have noticed that two themes run throughout the chapters in this book. First, in order to defrazzle our lives, we must become deliberate about our decisions. Second, as we attempt to lead our children into healthy adulthood, we are their role models. Believe it or not, that includes the fun factor. It can be as simple as a great jokebook at the dinner table or a full weekend of recreation just for the fun of it. Our plan in this chapter is to give you creative ideas to get you started and to spur you on to some great memories and healing laughter.

Six Strategies for Having More Family Time

- Watch the clock. This will help you know what time you have for important things like family.

- Do what you enjoy. A study that researched the lives of fourteen thousand families during the past twenty years found that people regularly overcommitted themselves to things they did not enjoy.

- Do not overbook your weekends. Much of our free time is lost while making the weekends a mad dash of to-dos. Try keeping an ongoing to-do list so things can be accomplished a little at a time.

- If you need help, do all you can to find it. If finances do not allow for this, try time exchanges with other moms or hiring an older high-school student or a retired neighbor when crunch times occur.

- Try not to plan every minute. Spontaneous fun can sometimes make for the best of times.

- Turn off the television. Lie on the floor and read together, play games, or do a puzzle. This type of focused energy makes for great conversation.

The ABCs of Fun

When you think of recreation, what comes to mind? Is it going to the fitness center to work out? Could it be playing softball with business associates or with family members? Maybe it is going to the park on a Sunday afternoon. The word *recreation* means to re-create oneself. To us that says refreshment, renewal, and enjoyment. We could all use a little re-creating, but we need to be deliberate about it or it won't happen.

Sometimes fun can be spontaneous, but the reality for us working moms is that if we are going to enjoy some re-creating time, we must intentionally plan fun and put it on the calendar. Maybe you'd like to play more often, but you don't have the creativity or energy to pursue it. Let's start with the ABCs of fun: *attitude, books,* and *communication.* Allow us to explain.

Attitude

In order to enjoy the fun of life, we must begin with our outlook. Are we willing to focus on the joyful side of circumstances,

Joy is the echo of God's life within us.

—Joseph Marmion

or are our eyes constantly diverted to the dread side? Attitude is a choice. Abraham Lincoln said, "Most folks are about as happy as they make up their minds to be."[2] Our attitude must be open to fun and the humor of life. We need to be willing to laugh at ourselves, be flexible in our circumstances, and give up some of the dogmatic ways we do things. Let's choose to see our world through the bright lenses of joy and gratitude rather than through the dark glasses of despair and grudges.

Books

Fulton Sheen said, "Books are the most wonderful friends in the world. When you meet them and pick them up, they are always ready to give you a few ideas."[3] We can gain many new and creative ideas on how to have fun from the wealth of books available to us. "I just don't have any fun ideas" should never be our excuse when there are so many creative books available. Take a lunch hour to visit a bookstore or library (or our favorite, discount or used bookstores) and pick up a boatload of fun ideas. You will open up a world of fun for your family through games and activities books, craft books, travel books, party books, and jokebooks. You are on your way to having fun because you have already begun with this book, and we will give you fun factor ideas later in this chapter.

Communication

Family fun doesn't just center around what *you* think is fun. Communication is a key element to good, hearty amusement. As you plan vacations or family outings, discuss what everyone would enjoy. We all see fun from different angles.

If you are going to the local fair, then communicate before you go in order to find out what everyone wants to do when you get there. One child may want to pet the animals, while another wants to ride the rides, while another family member wants to eat the food or play the games. Just make sure you do a little of each so that all family members know their voices were heard and can enjoy the entire time knowing they had the opportunity to do what they wanted to do. Younger ones may not be able to communicate in long sentences, but they will communicate when they are tired, hot, hungry, or frustrated.

> Time you enjoyed wasting is not wasted time.
> —T. S. Eliot

Although we do not cater to everyone's whims, we also don't want to force fun. Find the healthy balance through listening and communicating in love. Part of fun means a little self-sacrifice so that everyone has a great time.

Plans for Recreation

Now that you know the ABC essentials to planning fun and recreation for your family, we want to give you some ideas and strategies to help you add these elements to your life. Don't worry; we're not going to overwhelm you with impractical ideas that will only make you feel guilty for not doing them. Our desire is to give you simple plans to enjoy with your family and friends. Don't try to do them all. You are in the driver's seat; we are just providing some creative fuel. We would also love for you to share some of your favorite ideas with us (and other readers) on our web site: www.HighHeelsandHomeLife.com.

Family fun comes in many forms—birthday celebrations, seasonal and holiday memories, family vacations, or simply downtime at home. We are going to give you Top Ten lists to help you build memories and enjoy life with your family and friends in each area. We begin with some essential items you need for homespun fun.

> If you never have, you should. These things are fun and fun is good.
> —Dr. Seuss, *Oh, the Places You'll Go*

Top Ten Things to Have On Hand to Create an Atmosphere of Fun in Your Home

- Board games (such as Chutes and Ladders, Monopoly, Life, and Cranium)
- Joke and riddle books (we recommend *Nelson's Big Book of Laughter*)
- Craft items (paper, crayons, glue sticks, washable paint, sponges, etc.)
- Good food and drinks (a plentiful supply of the kids' favorite snacks)
- Fun movies (oldies as well as some current favorites)
- Sidewalk chalk (for outdoor fun, like hopscotch and foursquare)
- Balls (all shapes, sizes, and sports)

- Fun music (from latest hits to sing-along songs)

- Positive attitude and smiles

- Visitors (family, neighbors, and friends)

Top Ten Things to Do
Every Season of the Year

Winter Wonders

- Mall mania (Visit a local mall to see decorations, shop, do a scavenger hunt.)

- Movie night (Watch holiday favorites at home or go to the theater.)

- Christmas light drive (Everyone chooses a favorite neighborhood to visit.)

- Marshmallow land (Create a city using marshmallows and toothpicks.)

- Snowflake art (Remember the snowflakes you made out of paper in first grade?)

- Toy store shopping (Buy toys for charity and pick out a family game.)

- Hot chocolate and cookies night (Make treats and enjoy them as a family.)

- Favorite Christmas story (Play Christmas music and read your favorites.)

- Christmas program (Choose one that the entire family will enjoy.)

- Nursing home visit (Put on a play, sing some songs, or take homemade cookies to the patients allowed to have them.)

Spring Creations

- Fly kites. (Be brave and give it a try. You can do it!)

- Watch the clouds. (Get sleeping bags and pillows and lie down outside.)

- Take a walk in God's beautiful world. (Enjoy the flowers, birds, and butterflies.)

- Make tissue paper flowers. (Use pipe cleaners as stems and colored tissue as blooms.)

- Make and blow pinwheels. (Colorful wind makers are fun and a great way to cool off.)

- Plant an herb garden. (Watch it grow, cook with the herbs, or give herbs to friends.)

- Visit a local zoo or stables to enjoy God's creation through the animals.

- Go to a local arboretum or gardens in a community park. (Nothing says "spring" like a garden.)

- Plant your own garden. (Choose plants or paint clay pots together.)

- Go to an outdoor café for lunch or tea. (Take every advantage of alfresco dining.)

Super Summers

- Bubble fun (Buy a bottle of bubbles or make your own super bubble formula.)[4]

- Chalk talk (Sidewalk chalk offers simple, creative fun for hours.)

- Water parks or sprinklers (We all need some wet and wild fun.)

- Spray bottle wars (Fill empty spray bottles with water and squirt!)

- Art museums (Many museums feature special summer programs.)

- Library hour (Most libraries offer summer reading programs.)

- Miniature golf (Putt-putt golf is a great family outing.)

- Backyard sleepover (Tents are optional. Wish upon a star or an entire galaxy.)

- Homemade ice-cream taste-off (Invite friends over and ask them to bring an ice-cream freezer filled with their family's favorite blend.)

> He who does not get fun and enjoyment out of every day . . . needs to reorganize his life.
> —George Matthew Adams

- Road trip (Take a day trip to a nearby town or city and see the sights.)

Fall Fantasy

- Family hike (Collect various items, like pine cones, pods, leaves.)

- Tree bark rubbing (Hold paper to side of tree and rub with crayon.)

- Orange turkey (Use oranges, toothpicks, and gumdrops to create a great gobbler.)

- Corny mosaic (Using the different colored kernels, create a mosaic picture.)

- Visit a pumpkin patch (Allow each family member to choose one.)

- Silly pumpkin art (Glue on rolling eyes, draw a mouth and nose, and create hair using yarn, raffia, pipe cleaners, or craft feathers.)

- Farmers market (Find fresh produce as far as the eye can see.)

- Go on a hayride or visit a farm.

- Read about the Pilgrims and Native Americans.

- Cook favorite fall recipes together.

If you obey all the rules, you miss all the fun.
—Katharine Hepburn

Creative Birthday Celebrations

Creative parties make marvelous memories. We want to give you simple tips and helpful hints for planning a wonderful birthday celebration without adding anxiety to your busy life. Think of a birthday celebration as a gift you are giving the birthday child. You don't have to be the perfect party-planning queen to make a memorable event. You can create a special gathering on a small budget by keeping the plans simple and kid-friendly.

Top Ten Tips for Successful Birthday Parties for Kids

- Let the birthday child help you decide on a theme. Give him or her three choices from which to pick.

- Invite wisely. Keep the numbers smaller when the kids are young. Keep your sanity level in mind. Ask for friends or family members to help.

- Plan age-appropriate activities and games.

- Use simple games and plan more than you think you need. (Games always take a shorter amount of time than you think.)

- Gather all the nonperishable supplies one week prior to the party.

- Establish who will be the activity helper (an adult or teenager) and discuss his or her responsibilities prior to the party.

129

- Review party manners with your children prior to your guests' arrival.

- Focus more on the activities than on the décor.

- Understand that it is okay to just serve cake and ice cream.

- Open presents at the party in a fun yet organized way.

Happy Holidays

Holidays can be anything but simple; actually, the word *survival* comes to mind. We all know how quickly holidays can turn from happy to harried if we become stressed. One of the most important principles we can share with you to help you experience joy during the holidays is, "Do not compare with others." It is easy to look around and see what other people are doing (going to every Christmas festival in town, making elaborate gingerbread houses from scratch, having Christmas tea with daughters at the downtown hotel).

> Most people are about as happy as they make up their minds to be.
> —Abraham Lincoln

It is also easy to get lost in what people are giving. We see other mothers giving their kids gifts without limits or only the biggest and the best. If we compare ourselves and our families to others, we begin to feel inadequate, especially during the holidays.

Our solution is to put on your Son-glasses. Yes, we know it is winter, but you need your Son-glasses in order to guard your eyes from the glare of the glitter and gold. Protect your eyes from harmful rays of comparison in what others are doing this holiday season. When we put on our Son-glasses, we are really placing our focus on God's Son and the light He brings to our world. Keep your eyes on the path He has set before you and live your life, not a life that meets other people's expectations.

> My advice to you is not to inquire why or whither, but just enjoy your ice cream while it's on your plate.
> —Thornton Wilder

Here are a few ideas to help your seasons be merry and bright.

Top Ten Tips to Simplify Your Holidays

- List everything you feel you should do to make the holidays perfect. Cross out things you do out of guilt or obligation while leaving only the tasks motivated by genuine love and enthusiasm.

- Before the holidays arrive, decide on the three most important things you want to accomplish during the season.

- Let go of any and every holiday tradition that does not fit your family's needs or desires.

- If the thought of sending Christmas cards sends you over the holly-laden edge, try sending an e-card instead. Click and add fun pictures of the family.

- Remember, this time of the year should be fun and meaningful. List every simple and doable idea that fits your family's criteria.

- Make December 26 your biggest shopping day of the season for next year. Purchase cards, wrappings, holiday tea towels, themed sweaters, socks, or whatever you might need to stock a gift closet for next year.

- Collect favorite Christmas children's picture books throughout the year. Our favorites include

  - Angela Elwell Hunt, *The Tale of Three Trees* (Colorado Springs: Lion, 1989).

  - Chris Van Allsburg, *The Polar Express* (New York: Houghton Mifflin, 1985).

  - Jeff Brumbeau, *The Quiltmaker's Gift* (New York: Scholastic, 2001).

- Purchase or rent some of the best Christmas classics, like *White Christmas* or *Miracle on 34th Street*, and watch them while you wrap your gifts.

- Turn off all the lights except for those on the tree. Grab some big pillows, soft blankets, and warm cocoa and share favorite Christmas memories by the tree each night before bed.

- Donate time, gifts, or financial resources to Operation Christmas Child, Salvation Army, Angel Tree, or Toys for Tots. Focusing our attention on those less fortunate helps everyone involved.

Fantastic Family Vacations

Family vacations can create some of our fondest lifelong memories as well as build and strengthen family relationships. Unfortunately, it is easy for a family vacation to turn into the trip from you-know-where. To have the best time possible on your family vacations, we want to give you some helpful ideas and preparation pointers. But first, get out your calendar and make a plan for your next vacation. That's right; go get your calendar and plan it right now. If you don't plan your vacation now, other activities will distract you and keep you from your planning.

> Enjoy yourself. These are the "good old days" you're going to miss in the years ahead.
> —Anonymous

A family vacation doesn't have to be expensive or extensive. You can plan a wonderful, fun getaway just driving to the next town and staying in the Holiday Inn Express with the indoor pool for one night. What makes a family vacation special is not where you go or the money you spend, but rather the time you enjoy together, creating simple family fun.

Top Ten Tips for Fantastic Family Vacations

- Provide a "boredom buster" bag for each child. Give each child age-appropriate snacks and activities to do while on the plane or in the car (may include puzzle books, markers, small games, magazines, or books). Give the bags to your children just before they board.

- Allow the kids to be involved in the trip-planning

> When one door of happiness closes, another opens; but often we look so long at the closed door that we do not see the one which has opened for us.
> —Helen Keller

process. Give them an opportunity to say what they would like to do at the destination.

- Plan and purchase as much as possible ahead of time (rental car, dinner reservations, show and amusement park tickets, etc.).

- Show pictures to your children and tell them about the destination and/or the family members they will be seeing or meeting. Allow older kids to research fun things to do at the destination.

- Break up long car rides by planning fun stops along the way.

- Bring a computer or small DVD player in the car. But don't watch movies the entire time; allow some time for talking and visiting and playing games in the car.

- Allow a different family member to choose the restaurant each night.

- If you are staying in a condo, allow different family members to plan the meals and cook. Cook meals together for some good family fun.

- Bring crayons, paper, or small games into restaurants in case of long waits.

- Decide ahead of time to be content and not annoyed. Share the attitude!

Reflecting on Fun

Musician and author Sheila Walsh places a high priority on pit stops of joy in her life. Here's what she has to say:

> If you're speeding down the freeway, the police might pull you over. But no one ever makes you take pit stops. You have to choose them. It's the same with life. Emergencies force us to stop, but pit stops of joy are events we plan for and savor. It's good to let go and to bring a little relief into the noise when life is clamoring at you.[5]

Fun, recreation, and play are vital components to weave into our lives. Encouraging our children's creativity offers us a chance to help them reach greater heights. It gives us moms another way to connect and bond with our children.

What was the best fun you had with your family when you were growing up?

_____

_____

What was your best family celebration?

_____

Re-create with your own children what worked well in your family of origin. Remember, now it is your opportunity to build fond memories for your family. Keep in mind that deliberate does it. Plan fun activities and events, or they won't happen.

It is a happy
talent to know
how to play.
—Ralph Waldo
Emerson

Take a moment before you move on to the next chapter to circle one activity listed in this chapter that you will do in the coming month. Jot down a date beside it and make it happen.

Most important, enjoy the people God has put into your life! Smile at one another, laugh together, and make every occasion a great occasion when you are together with your kids and friends.

We close this chapter with a story by Gloria Gaither, reflecting on a simple lesson of joy:

Recently I stopped for breakfast at the local pancake house. I intended to steal a moment to be alone before the day began and its many demands crowded my time. "Just an egg and homemade biscuit," I told the waitress. "And a coffee, please." I handed back the menu and turned to the book I'd brought to jump-start my mind. I had barely finished the second page before she returned with my breakfast.

She poured the coffee and asked if there'd be anything else. "No, I'm fine, thank you," I answered. She smiled. "Enjoy!" she said, then hurried back to deliver someone else's order. Her final word hung in the air above my corner booth like a blessing. It was a choice she had offered me I could go through this day oblivious to the miracles all around me or I could tune in and "enjoy!"

I've heard a lot of sermons in my day, but the best sermon I'd heard in a long time was preached in one word by a busy waitress as she poured a cup of coffee. God has given us this day. I don't want to miss it. Enjoy![6]

The Fun Factor at a Glance

- Fun is a recess from the responsibilities of life.

- What foils our fun? Often it can be poor time management, an overly serious attitude, or the burdens of business.

- The word *recreation* means to re-create oneself. To us that includes refreshment, renewal, and enjoyment.

- Parents who encourage their child's creativity have an opportunity to learn about their child's thinking process.

- Use the seasonal suggestions for fun activities, crafts, and places to go as a starting place for family fun.

- Celebrate birthdays, holidays, and special days in a fun and simple way.

The ABCs of Fun

- Attitude—Choose to focus on the joyful side of circumstances.

- Books—Learn new and creative ideas for fun by reading books.

- Communication—As you plan vacations or family outings, discuss what everyone would enjoy.

meditations
for the frazzled soul

You have filled my heart with greater joy than when their grain and new wine abound.

PSALM 4:7 NIV

Your statutes are my heritage forever; they are the joy of my heart.

PSALM 119:111 NIV

The prospect of the righteous is joy, but the hopes of the wicked come to nothing.

PROVERBS 10:28 NIV

If you have any encouragement from being united with Christ, if any comfort from his love, if any fellowship with the Spirit, if any tenderness and compassion, then make my joy complete by being likeminded, having the same love, being one in spirit and purpose.

PHILIPPIANS 2:1–2 NIV

But may the righteous be glad and rejoice before God; may they be happy and joyful.

PSALM 68:3 NIV

A happy heart makes the face cheerful, but heartache crushes the spirit.

PROVERBS 15:13 NIV

Saving herself hours of cleanup time, Carol wisely outfitted Justin with a personal toy rake.

chapter 6

The Rejuvenation Factor
Taking Time for Personal Refreshment

*If we could learn how to balance rest against effort,
calmness against strain, quiet against turmoil, we
would assure ourselves of joy in living and
psychological health for life.*

—JOSEPHINE RATHBONE

Yeah right, Sandra thought as she listened to Mr. Seminar give his corporate presentation esteeming the virtues of a balanced life and the importance of taking care of oneself.

How does one actually do that? Sandra mused. Between her full-time job as an administrative assistant and her online courses to finish her teaching degree, Sandra barely had time to care for the needs of her three children, much less think about herself.

So when does a working mom have "mommy time"? How can she refresh herself? Is it possible? Yes it is, and we want to provide realistic ways to do it!

This chapter brings you soothing hope. Although we cannot step out of the pages of this book and help you do the laundry or assist you with the kids, we can give you some practical ways to refresh yourself in the midst of the responsibilities you carry. Our desire is to replenish you mentally, physically, spiritually, and emotionally. We also want to give you some timesaving tips to help you make the most of your time. As we present the possibilities for nourishment and growth, we encourage you to do what you can, when you can. Take the opportunity to refresh your soul in simple ways as you relax and read this refreshing chapter.

Filling Up Your Emotional Tank

You give a lot. You give of yourself mentally and emotionally at work. You give of yourself physically and emotionally at home. Emotionally speaking, your tank can become empty and yet often you may not have time or the means to fill it. What can you do? We want to give you several solutions in order to help refuel your emotional tank. Although you may already be aware of some of these solutions, we want to remind you to deliberately apply them. In driving a car, it's easy to forget to look at the gas gauge, and before you know it, you are on empty. We want to remind you to check your emotional gas gauge before it is empty, and we hope to give you some fuel to help you fill up emotionally.

Fueling Your Friendships

God created us as relational beings. Often a listening ear or the shoulder of an encouraging friend to hug can take the edge off our emotions. If you are married, you cannot and should not depend on your husband alone to fill up your emotional tank. He is not equipped to do so (although he may be there for you at times). Even your friends cannot meet all of your needs, but they can give you that boost you need to stay on track.

If you find it difficult to find a time to meet with a good friend, consider other friendship options that could work in your life. What about a mentor with a flexible schedule? Perhaps there is a wise woman you know, one who has shared some of the same beliefs and struggles. Perhaps you can ask her to join you for lunch. You may want to set a once-a-month time to get together so you can be an encouragement to one another.

> Concentrate on the issues that are most important to you and minimize or ignore the non-essentials.
> —James C. Numan

We have found in our own lives that it helps to set a regular time to meet with certain friends, or the days and weeks will get away from us and it is easy to drift away. Think right now of a friend (or even an acquaintance) whom you find refreshing, someone who encourages you and strengthens you and makes you feel like a better person. Plan to give that person a call this week to set a time to get together, and see if she is willing to meet once a month. Hopefully you will be just as refreshing to her as she is to you.

Support groups are good places to begin a friendship or find encouragement from another person. There are a variety of different ways to find the common bond of support that you need. One such way is through a working mother's online support group. Using an e-mail loop or bulletin board, you can ask questions and find answers daily by staying in e-contact with other women who know what your life is like. You can visit our web site (www.HighHeelsandHomeLife.com) to connect with other working moms.

Journaling Your Thoughts

There are times when it helps to get your thoughts and emotions out of your head and onto paper. Journaling can help you write out your questions, your anger, and your frustrations. It can also help you plan your strategies and see things more clearly.

Blank journals are easy to find, and you can fill them with the cries of your heart or the joy of your soul. There is no right or wrong way to journal; just do what seems natural for you. You may want to read a scripture and then write down your thoughts about what God is teaching you. You may want to write out a prayer or a concern that you want to give over to God.

> We need time to dream, time to remember, and time to reach the infinite. Time to be.
> —Gladys Taber

Journaling is not an answer to all your troubles, but it does help you smooth out your emotions and organize your thinking.

Casting Your Cares

The Bible tells us to cast our cares on the Lord, for He cares for us (see 1 Peter 5:7). Often we tend to hold in or hide our cares, trying to give the appearance that we have it all together. We all do it in some way or another, yet there is no greater relief than giving our worries over to Him through prayer. "Lord, I'm scared. I am afraid _____ will happen. Please replace my fear with peace."

"Lord, I'm angry because _____. Please help me to calm down and to forgive."

We can take our emotions to God because He cares for us! It is amazing that the God of all creation wants us to go to Him. It's also amazing how easily we forget to give Him our cares and concerns.

Is there anything you are holding on to in your heart that is draining you emotionally? Why don't you stop reading right now, bow your head, and give that situation or emotion over to God?

Now don't try to take back your cares once you have given them to God. Yes, you can continue to pray about them, but don't continue to let them fester and build up into an emotional volcano. Receive His emotional healing as you cast your cares daily at His feet.

Seeing a Counselor

There are times when we may need feedback beyond a friend's caring words. You may want to seek a professional counselor through your church or the recommendation of a trusted friend. We strongly encourage you to find a Bible-based counselor. God's Word offers us a foundation of truth, and you want to visit a counselor who uses Scripture as his or her primary source to help you through your struggles. You may find that a professional counselor will help you understand some of your emotions and help you work through struggles to a point of solution.

Victoria is in the prime of a strenuous yet exciting career as a news reporter, and she is also a mother of one very involved child. During the past several years, she has been dealing with an avalanche of emotions. Her mother is dying. Her father is not well either, often lashing out at Victoria with unpredictable behaviors, causing undue emotional

> If you don't like who you are and where you are, don't worry about it, because you're not stuck either with who you are or where you are. You can grow. You can change. You can be more than you are.
> —Zig Ziglar

stress. After discussing some of her deep family issues with friends and mentors, Victoria was encouraged to seek the wisdom of a Bible-based counselor. She did.

As she began to describe her turmoil, Victoria felt that her counselor really listened. The process of talking through her concerns allowed her the opportunity to think through each circumstance. The godly feedback from her counselor helped her see how she could better deal with the uncertain behaviors and her feelings of deep sorrow. "It felt like a spiritual and emotional spring-cleaning," described Victoria. "The problems were still alive and well, but my ability to see my choices within my personal realities allowed me to view my life with a clearer vision." Going to a professional counselor is not a sign of weakness; rather, a counselor can help us better our understanding and strengthen our resolve to press on to our God-given purpose.

Taking Time for Physical Refreshment

When you applied for motherhood, did you read in the job description that it was a physically demanding job? Yes, it was right there nestled in with midnight feedings and cleaning up muddy sneakers. Add your career to the top of that list and you have a good reason to be, let's just say, slightly worn out. Here are some thoughts to help you refresh yourself physically. These tips may not all work for you, but pick a few that may fit into your lifestyle.

It's not so much how busy you are, but why you are so busy. The bee is praised; the mosquito is swatted.
—Marie O'Conner

Once-a-Month Gift to Yourself

Take a moment to consider what would really be physically relaxing to you personally. We're talking about some activity that you could really look forward to as a gift for yourself. Some say a massage or maybe a long walk in the park. Other moms would enjoy a hot bubble bath or even a pedicure. Write down in the margin of this book one thing that would truly refresh you. It must be practical and affordable.

Ten Ways to Pamper Yourself

- Take a long walk in a beautiful place.

- Relax in a hot bubble bath surrounded by candles.

- Get a manicure or pedicure.

- Snuggle in an oversized bathrobe with a cup of coffee and a good book.

- Call a friend just to laugh together.

- Purchase lip liner and lipstick in the season's new color.

- Schedule an afternoon at your favorite bookstore.

- Place a vase of fresh flowers by your bedside.

- Take a plunge in a cool pool on a scorching day.

- Buy a refreshing fragrance.

Now get out your calendar and schedule it. That's right—find a day this month that you can give yourself a treat, and write it down. You may need to do it when your kids are at school or ballet or when they are with their dad, but even if it is a walk in the park, you need to put it on the calendar or it won't happen. Continue this practice every month. It will be your special treat to look forward to each month. Even when life gets tough, you know that you have your treat waiting for you around the corner. We all need a little motivation to make it through.

Good-Night Glory

Although it's not always easy to get a good night's sleep, we must never underestimate its benefit. Let's review what we are doing in the evening to see if there is any way to cut out an unnecessary activity (say, a television show or reading a magazine) to get to bed just a little earlier. Perhaps you are a dawdler like we are. Like us, you're always piddling around getting five more things done before you go to bed. Here's an idea: set a kitchen timer to go off so that it can be that voice to remind you like your mother did: "Go to bed!"

It may be possible for you to grab a short power nap during the day. A little nap can do a lot of good. Harvard University researchers found that a midday snooze reverses information overload. They also found that people could improve their motor skills 20 percent by getting a few extra winks in the morning. The bottom line: we should stop feeling guilty about taking a "power nap" at work or catching extra winks the night before a big presentation. The brain uses a night's sleep to consolidate the memories of habits, actions, and skills learned during the day.

The researchers found that burnout—irritation, frustration, and poorer performance on a mental task—sets in as a day of training wears on. But a thirty-minute nap during a day of work stopped the progression of burnout in study participants, and a one-hour nap boosted the performance of the worker.[1]

Café Energy

It's so easy to ignore the fact that the food we eat gives our bodies the fuel we need to keep up the pace. Take a deliberate look at what you are eating. Consider eating less sugar, white flour, and saturated fats. Take a good multivitamin, and eat foods that build you up rather than drain you. We know it seems simple, but what you put in your mouth affects your ability to handle the pressures of life both physically and emotionally. Eat well and live well.

Workable Workout

Clinical evidence demonstrates that "the body increases the production of endorphins after 20 minutes or more of exercise. Chemically this is similar to the opiates found in morphine-like substances. These endorphins can have a pain relieving effect and can promote a mental state of euphoria. The positive mood associated from frequent exercising effectively reduces depression and stress-related problems."[2] There are volumes of articles touting the physical and emotional benefits of exercise. To truly take care of yourself, exercise must become part of your routine.

You may only have time to walk the stairs in your building or take a walk at lunch, but every bit really does count. Just three times a week can be a benefit to you. But you don't have to go to the workout facility to get your workout in. Here are some possibilities to mesh exercise into your daily routine to help keep you fit.

- Park farther away from your office or get off one bus stop early. Use the long walk as an opportunity to get some exercise and as a time to think and pray through the concerns of the day.
- Take the stairs rather than the elevator.
- Do a workout video at home with the kids. At certain ages, some kids find it fun to do the workout routines. Try Leslie Sansone's Walk for Life videos. They are uplifting workouts by a fellow Christian.
- Work out while watching television with the family. Do the bicycle, leg lifts, tummy crunches, stretches, etc.
- Find a workout buddy (someone who enjoys the same type of exercise you do). Set a time to work out together at least once a week.

Looking Your Best

Under the umbrella of taking care of ourselves physically comes the element of looking our best and presenting an attractive appearance. Clothes, makeup, and hairstyle all work together to create a confident reflection of you. Here are several tips to help you look tremendous at work and at home.

Makeup

Use makeup only to enhance your natural beauty, not to overtake your appearance. Consider having your makeup done by a cosmetic representative to find the colors that work best for you. Your blush color and lip color should be in the same color family. (Remember, not all lipstick colors look the same on all women.)

Skin

Take good care of your skin. Choose a water-based moisturizer. Get in the habit of using a good cleansing mask. Use sunscreen. Drink six to eight glasses of water a day. Check out several skin-care lines to find the one that works best with your skin.

Clothes

When shopping for new clothes, stay in the range of colors that look best on you. Monochrome (especially black) is slimming and will stay in style longer than prints. Buy clothes that diminish your negative qualities and accentuate your positive ones. Know your own personal style (classic/conservative, casual/natural, or high fashion), and stick with it. If you are on a tight budget, just update your wardrobe with accessories to add a new interest and flair. For work, purchase coordinating basics and separates so you can have many different looks using several blouses and a few basic pants or skirts.

Hairstyle

Update your hairstyle every few years. Look for styles on other women and in magazines. Consider the shape of your face and look especially for those hairstyles that enhance your shape and lifestyle.

Twelve Ways to Streamline
and Style-Up Your Wardrobe

- Perform a closet inventory. Divide a notebook into sections for blouses, pants, and so on. List what you have and give away what you never wear. Take this notebook with you when you shop to help you remember what you do and do not need.

- Purchase a string of pearls. They don't have to be real, just elegant. Pearls are stylish with jeans as well as that perfect black dress.

- Purchase several sweater sets in solid colors to wear with alternating skirts and pants. The shell part of the set looks great under a jean jacket.

- Invest extra money in wardrobe staples, such as black pants, a black skirt, crisp white blouses, and a navy blazer.

- Update your accessories. Keep the design simple yet classic.

- Consider these things when you are reviewing your wardrobe: your lifestyle, your personal style, your body style, and your comfort.

- Make sure to always have a crisp white shirt ready. It's good with jeans, khakis, a black skirt, and a blazer.

- Ask a style-conscious friend to keep you in the fashion loop. Just because you are juggling the world does not mean you can't look good.

- Each quarter do a quick style research. The magazine *InStyle* does a rundown on each season's must-haves. Now, it is up to you to make sure you really need the "must-haves," but this will at least give you a style overview of each season.

- Shop via mail-order catalogs and web sites of your favorite stores. Shopping from home will reduce shopping time and style concerns—take a quick look, order, and be fashionable.

- Buy quality clothes in monochromatic colors to stretch your wardrobe.

- Make sure your selections are travel-friendly. Ironing can be a real drag after a long travel day and before an early-morning meeting.

Confidence

Confidence is a look. The more you act confident, the more you feel confident. How do you look confident? Begin with your posture. "Sit up straight, shoulders back, stomach in, and don't slouch!" Can't you just hear your mom instructing you to improve your posture? Other signs of confidence are shown in your smile, eye contact, and the way you walk. Make a conscious effort to pay attention to the message you are presenting. Be confident and be the best you!

Staying Mentally Strong

Would you consider yourself a learner? Whether or not you enjoy learning, you can always add to your knowledge for personal growth, professional growth, or simply staying current with political and social issues. Here are several easy ways to stay on top of the mental game:

- Listen to motivational messages or books on tape during your travel time to and from work. You can even learn a new language if you feel so inclined.

- Attend a professional workshop or convention at least once a year.

- Find a good news station (radio or television) and listen to it while you are getting ready in the morning.

- Determine a fair and reasonable goal for reading a book (one book per month, one book every two months, etc.).

- Read while you eat during one lunch hour each week.

- Learn the art of skimming. As you glance at the newspaper, read the headlines and skim for key details. Highlight any articles you want to come back to later. For magazines, skim the contents page and tear out any articles that you want to read. Throw away the magazine and read or file the ones you pulled out. Often you can briefly skim the contents of a nonfiction book to get the most important points, then carefully read the chapters in which you need more information.

English poet Joseph Addison once said, "Reading is to the mind what exercise is to the body." This was one of Mary Beth's favorite quotes, but it took her years to really believe it. Why? She was such a visual learner. She loved looking at the pictures in books; in fact, she would often learn more from the illustrations than the words. The pictures were interesting because she was a slow reader, taking in every word. In school as well as in business, reading is a vital component for gaining knowledge and learning new skills, which were both important to Mary Beth. Increasing her reading speed and mental acuity became a project. The library became a place not only of quiet but a place to research and become an expert. Get smart.

Whatever the topic, Mary Beth would select several books to review: first the back cover, then the contents page, next a skim of the first and last chapters. If this book still piqued her interest, she would check it out. Today, when time is a limited commodity, her book-selecting system is the same. Mary Beth found what worked best for her, and we encourage you to find what works for you. Remember, a good mind is a terrible thing to waste.

Spiritual Stamina

Ever feel like you just can't keep a consistent prayer life? Author Cheri Fuller recalls a significant discovery she made in her own life concerning prayer: "I used to think, *If I don't pray at a certain time of day, then my prayers don't really count.* Then my prayer life underwent a radical transformation. I discovered the apostle Paul's command to 'pray continually' (1 Thessalonians 5:17 NIV) means more than just spending a lot of time in prayer; it means sharing a continual dialogue with God wherever I go."[3]

Our prayer lives can flourish as we walk and talk with God throughout the day. Certainly it is helpful to have a steady time alone to meet with the Lord, just as we know Jesus did (see Mark 1:35). Starting our day with a time of solitude with God can be just the rejuvenation we need to face the day, but it may not always happen in the typical, busy morning rush. Instead of feeling guilty about it, point your thoughts heavenward throughout the day. The apostle Paul wrote, "Since, then, you have been raised with Christ, set your hearts on things above, where Christ is seated at the right hand of God" (Colossians 3:1 NIV).

We don't want to lose our focus on God when we leave church on Sunday mornings. We can continually keep our hearts and minds pointed heavenward in an abiding relationship with God. God encourages us to ask, seek, and knock (see Matthew 7:7). He wants us to spend time with Him because He desires a relationship with us. That is truly amazing to think about! The God of the universe wants to draw close to His creation in a loving relationship. So we seek to have alone time with our loving heavenly Father, but we can also keep our hearts and minds pointed to Him throughout the day.

Fellowship with God, fellowship with other believers, and the fellowship of God's Word all help us to stay spiritually strong. If you don't have the opportunity to be around other Christians in the workplace, look for other opportunities to develop relationships with believers. Take your kids to Sunday school, then find an adult class to visit. Good fellowship with other Christians usually doesn't take place in the worship service, but rather during

Sunday school or other small groups. If your kids go to church activities on a weeknight, then look for an adult gathering or agree to meet one of the parents for coffee during that time.

There is great spiritual refreshment in the Word of God. You can grow in your knowledge of God's Word in small, bite-size nuggets. One idea is to slowly read through the Bible, taking a few verses or a chapter at a time. Then write in a journal about what you read and what you learn. Make a note of how the passage can apply to your life personally. A good study Bible has helpful notes that relate to many of the verses. Remember, investing in your spiritual growth is always time well spent.

Victory over the Battle for Your Time

As we recognize the benefits for rejuvenating the various aspects of our lives, a very real and pressing issue is figuring out how to fit all we need to do into our overloaded schedule. How can we best use the twenty-four hours God has given us each day?

One of the first things we need to do to get control of our time is to identify the things that steal our time. Here are some of our common time robbers. See if you can identify with any of these time snatchers:

- Making midday phone calls with excess conversation
- Hovering over e-mail and then checking it again just in case something important came in
- Surfing the Internet
- Hopping from task to task, never quite completing anything

- Taking too many trips to the grocery store and spending too much time figuring out what's for dinner
- Watching too much TV in the evening
- Running unconsolidated errands
- Looking for the lost file in a stack of to-dos
- Being distracted by a magazine or book or story
- Chitchatting at the office or two-hour lunches

Write your top time waster in the space below or circle any of the ones above that apply to your typical day.

_____

It's also important to point out some useful and important activities that we might, in our zealousness to get control of our time, mislabel as time wasters. Here are some things we need to keep on the agenda:

- Playtime with our kids or interruptions by them
- Dates with husband and friends
- Exercise time
- Devotional and Bible study time
- A few minutes of downtime each day for reading or relaxing

The challenge is to weed out the unnecessary time robbers and to focus more deliberately on the activities that have value in our lives. If you are like us, you have at least three time-management and organizational books on your shelf. They can really be helpful—if you put their strategies to work. Otherwise, they can be time robbers as much as anything else. We're going to boil down some of the most common advice in the books in hopes of saving you a little time!

> When your schedule leaves you drained and stressed to exhaustion, it's time to give up something. Delegate. Say no. It's like cleaning out a closet: After a while it gets easier to get rid of things. You discover that you really didn't need them anyway.
> —Marilyn Ruman

- Determine your priorities and schedule your time around your priorities.

- Minimize interruptions. Focus on valuable communication first.

- Keep your to-do list reasonable. Rank items with ABC importance.

- Try to complete one task before starting another.

- Plan ahead. Determine the next day's priorities the night before.

We could spend hours talking about the philosophy of time management or discussing big-picture timesaving strategies like those above. We don't know about you, but what we really need is usable in-the-trench-type tips, so let's get down to the nitty-gritty, timesaving essentials for a working mom.

- Prepare lunches in the evenings before school days.

- For younger kids, lay out or organize their clothes for the week on Sunday night.

- Display a large calendar on the kitchen wall and write everyone's activities on it for all to see.

- Keep an organizer or PDA with you at all times and use it constantly. Keep important phone numbers with you at all times.

- Streamline grocery shopping by creating a master list of typical items your family uses. Type it up and put it in a plastic cover (or laminate it), then use a wipe-off marker to mark the items you need each week. Or better yet, if it is available in your area, order your groceries online for home delivery.

- Write down your shopping list in the order of the supermarket layout. You'll never have to double back.

- Use a Crockpot as often as possible.

- Keep a list of phone numbers of your favorite restaurants for takeout orders.

- On the weekends, prepare several dinners and put them in the freezer for the following week.

- When making a casserole for dinner, double the recipe and put half in the freezer for another meal.

- Have a ten-minute cleanup time after dinner each night. The entire family picks up and straightens for just ten minutes; this keeps the house amazingly neat.

- Have one place for bills and keep them there. Choose two days a month for paying bills (such as the tenth and the twenty-fifth), and stick to it.

- Spend seven minutes each morning cleaning a bathroom. It's amazing how little time it takes to swish and wipe a toilet, swab the sink, and polish the mirror.

- Try to do one load of laundry every day—wash, fold, and put away. With towels and sheets, you can easily find a load for each day, and you won't get behind.

- Develop routines that you will stick to. For example, have a before-bed routine that includes laying out everyone's clothes, preparing for tomorrow's dinner (get food out of the freezer), and cleaning the kitchen. In the morning, make the beds, wipe the bathroom, throw in a load of laundry, and plan for the next day.

- On Saturday morning, do a quick wallet check to make sure you have the cash your family needs for the next week. Put the kids' lunch money in envelopes labeled for each day.

- Plan ahead for children's dawdling time, trying to be realistic about how much time it takes them to get dressed, brush their teeth, eat breakfast, and so on.

- Reassess your family's activities. Don't try to keep up with the Joneses (just because everyone else puts their child in soccer at age three doesn't mean you should). Only do the activities that are right for your family.

- Use your commute time to and from work to return phone calls or catch up on some reading with books on tape.

- Designate one lunch hour a week to run errands (post office, cleaners, store, etc.).

A Radical, Ancient Idea

When it comes to refreshing and rejuvenating our souls, our Creator knows what we need. He set a lifestyle pattern for humanity, and it was a pattern He practiced Himself in the process of creation. God felt so strongly about this lifestyle pattern that He put it in the Ten Commandments. Number Four of the Big Ten says, "Remember to observe the Sabbath day by keeping it holy. Six days a week are set apart for your daily duties and regular work, but the seventh day is a day of rest dedicated to the LORD your God" (Exodus 20:8–10).

The word *sabbath* means to cease or desist. It refers to a cessation from activity. God intended for this to be a day set aside for rest and worship. He knew we needed to be deliberate about setting aside unhurried time, or it simply wouldn't happen. This commandment shows how wonderful our God's care is for us. By commanding that His people set aside one day a week as a day for rest and worship, He was not giving them a burden, but rather a gift. God, who made us and knows us, knows we function best when we follow a plan for intentional rest.

How do you actually take a Sabbath rest? Let's look at it step by step. First, we need to determine in our hearts that this is a way of life worth pursuing. One day of worship and rest doesn't mean we will spend the morning at church and then come home and lay around for the rest of the day, lazily doing nothing. It does mean that we plan to set aside this day as different. Six days of the week we do our work and home responsibilities, and one day a week we set aside to recoup, regroup, and worship the Lord. It is a day to stop normal activities and to rest and refresh.

> Insanity
> is doing the same
> thing over and over
> again but expecting
> different results.
> —Rita Mae Brown

Now, we know it may be impossible to cut away every activity on the Sabbath, and we certainly don't want to be legalistic about strictly doing nothing. All we want to do is encourage you to slow down and change directions on that day, letting it become a day of refreshment. Here's a practical way to play it out:

- *Let your family know that you want to do things differently.* Tell them you plan to cease from work (which can mean business work and/or housework) one day a week.

- *Worship the Lord.* He has given us six days of the week to do what we need to do. It's not too hard to devote several hours to Him one day a week.

- *Determine what is truly restful to you.* It may be a nap. It could be reading a book or taking a walk or going on a bike ride. Rest may come in the form of not answering the phone and not checking e-mail. You may find it helpful to use a part of the day to pray through issues or plan out your week.

The Balance of It All

It seems as though the term *balanced life* is more of an oxymoron than a plausible reality. Life is full of changes, challenges, and inequities. Just as we tell our kids, "Life isn't fair," we need to also remind ourselves that "Life doesn't balance." Our job is not to continually live in frustration because we cannot achieve the perfect balance of family, work, and personal growth. What we can do with life's inequities is to be flexible, grow with the changes, and reevaluate on a regular basis.

> Finish every day and be done with it. You have done what you could. Some blunders and absurdities no doubt crept in; forget them as soon as you can. Tomorrow is a new day. Begin it well.
>
> —Ralph Waldo Emerson

We may not be able to be on top of our game mentally, physically, spiritually, and emotionally all at the same time, but we can make sure we are growing in each area even in small doses. There may be times in our lives when we are really working out and staying fit, then there are other times when this area may dwindle to a brisk walk two times a week. We don't want to let any area go undeveloped, because they all work together in harmony to make us who we are.

Personal restoration comes when we give attention to each of these areas. One area may get more attention than the other for a period of time, but always look to see that you are not letting an area of your life completely waste away through inattentiveness. You may even want to write on an index card these words: *mental, physical, spiritual,* and *emotional.* Determine how you plan to grow in or maintain each of these areas and write a brief description. Place the card where you keep your bills. Each month when you pay your bills, read the card as a way of self-check to make sure you are taking care of yourself.

Remember, you are the best you that you can give your family. Take care of yourself so you can give your best.

The Rejuvenation Factor at a Glance

- Become intentional about taking a day of rest each week.

- Worship God.

- Stay filled emotionally through friendships, journaling, casting your cares on Jesus, and when necessary, seeking a counselor's touch.

- The benefits of physical exercise are incredible. Find what works for you.

- Watch what you eat! Your food choices can make a difference in your energy level.

- Talk with God all day long; pray for wisdom at home, at work, in every aspect of life.

- Personal restoration is achieved when we pay attention to the spiritual, physical, mental, and emotional aspects of our lives.

- Flexibility + personal reassessment + self-care = balance

- Take care of you so you can take care of everything else.

meditations
for the frazzled soul

Physical
So whether you eat or drink or whatever you do, do it all for the glory of God.

1 CORINTHIANS 10:31 NIV

Mental
Finally, brothers, whatever is true, whatever is noble, whatever is right, whatever is pure, whatever is lovely, whatever is admirable—if anything is excellent or praiseworthy—think about such things.

PHILIPPIANS 4:8 NIV

The discerning heart seeks knowledge, but the mouth of a fool feeds on folly.

PROVERBS 15:14 NIV

Emotional
Cast all your anxiety on him because he cares for you.

1 PETER 5:7 NIV

Spiritual

Very early in the morning, while it was still dark, Jesus got up, left the house and went off to a solitary place, where he prayed.

MARK 1:35 NIV

Personal

Teach me your way, O LORD, and I will walk in your truth.

PSALM 86:11 NIV

Teach us to make the most of our time, so that we may grow in wisdom.

PSALM 90:12

Remember to observe the Sabbath day by keeping it holy. Six days a week are set apart for your daily duties and regular work, but the seventh day is a day of rest dedicated to the LORD your God.

EXODUS 20:8–10

As a service to mothers, school buses at
Douglasville School District were outfitted
with forgotten-item retrieval bins.

chapter 7

The Grace Factor
Walking in God's Abundance

They travel lightly whom God's grace carries.

THOMAS À KEMPIS

Perform. Perform. Perform.

Do you sometimes feel like your life is all about performance? We have to do a near-perfect job at work in order to please the boss or get the client's approval. At home we stretch ourselves to be everything we can be for our children, helping them to feel nurtured and loved so they will grow up to be healthy, well-balanced, responsible adults. At church we give our time, talents, and money in order to be considered a "good church member." Then there's our desire to be a "good wife," a "good neighbor," a "good daughter," and a "good friend"—the list is endless.

Life on the performance treadmill can be tiring. Granted, there are many areas of life that require us to do our work with excellence, as well we should. Then there are other areas in which we continually perform, not because we must but because we think we must. And it's easy to forget that we are not on the performance treadmill when it comes to our relationship with God. Jesus said, "Come to Me, all you who labor and are heavy laden, and I will give you rest. Take My yoke upon you and learn from Me, for I am gentle and lowly in heart, and you will find rest for your souls. For My yoke is easy and My burden is light" (Matthew 11:28–30 NKJV). That's an invitation to step off the performance treadmill if we've ever heard one!

God's grace gives us relief and refreshment from our workaholic world. Instead of saying, "You must work your way to heaven," God says, "By grace you have been saved through faith" (Ephesians 2:8 NKJV). Instead of saying, "I will only use you if you are perfect," God says, "My grace is sufficient for you, for my power is made perfect in weakness" (2 Corinthians 12:9 NIV). Instead of holding our mistakes and sins against us, God says, "As far as the east is from the west, so far [have I] removed [your] transgressions from [you]" (Psalm 103:12 NKJV).

Yes, God's grace looks different than the systems of this world. When we fully embrace the beauty of God's grace, we find a spiritual renewal that permeates every area of our lives. The first step to dwelling in His grace is getting to know this glorious God who so freely offers His grace.

Understanding God

In many areas of life, we can manage our outcomes. "If I do X, the outcome will be Y." God's economy works a little differently. As much as we would love to be in charge, God (who is in charge) is neither manageable nor predictable. It's humbling but true that we can't figure out God, which helps us recognize that God is God and we are not.

Yet it's easy to think that if I act a certain way or am basically good, everything will go smoothly in my life and God will answer all my prayers the way I want. Take Rhonda for instance.

She struggled with her understanding of God. "If God really loved me, I would not have been overlooked for a promotion. I've been good and gone to church every Sunday. Why didn't He reward my effort?" Rhonda believed that if she performed well, God would reward her with good things and everything would work out the way she thought it should. But God doesn't define Himself by making life easy for all who will follow Him. Sometimes His followers go through trials, challenges, and pain. Sometimes they suffer for doing the right thing.

Take Paul for instance. He was beaten and imprisoned for preaching the good news about Jesus. Now if God were a God who gives His good performers only good things, then Paul would have had a cushy life. Instead, he suffered greatly for the gospel's sake. Yet Paul had a powerful and positive impact on the early Christians, and he still does on us today. The suffering Paul endured matured him, humbled him, and helped him rely on God and not himself.

We must come to grips with the fact that God is not a performance-based God. While good works are part of our Christian life, they are not the "currency" needed to purchase our redemption. That would be like taking Monopoly money to Neiman Marcus. If we do all the good, "God-pleasing" things we can do, He doesn't necessarily reward us with good times, mega-money, perfect kids, or a promotion. If that were the case, then all of the prophets and leaders in the Bible would have had heaven on earth! God doesn't promise us good stuff and earthly blessings. He does promise His faithfulness and love. He promises to be with us through life's disappointments, challenges, and successes.

One of the most important things we can understand about

God is that we can't understand God. His ways are not our ways, and His thoughts are not our thoughts (see Isaiah 55:8–9). The entire book of Job points to the fact that God's ways don't always make sense to us. Job was doing everything right—walking in obedience to God—yet his world fell apart. As we read the book of Job, we are allowed to see that there was a bigger, spiritual battle going on—but Job couldn't see the bigger picture. He questioned God, as we would most likely do. God lovingly answered. He reminded Job that He was in charge and that Job couldn't possibly comprehend all that was going on. God said, "Where were you when I laid the foundations of the earth? Tell Me, if you have understanding" (Job 38:4 NKJV).

> Religion in its humility restores man to his only dignity, the courage to live by grace.
> —George Santayana

The message was clear. God is the creator of the world. He knows what He is doing because He is an all-wise God. We can trust His love, even when we do not have a full understanding of His ways. The tough part for us to swallow is that bad things happen to good people and good things happen to bad people. We don't like that. It doesn't equate with how we would run the world.

Although it sounds difficult and even confusing, faith is actually freeing. God's not going to make us lose our job because we missed church for three weeks. He's not going to zap us with a tax audit just because we raised our voices to our kids. Now we're not saying that gives us the right to live our lives with reckless abandon. No, there are natural consequences to our actions, and God gives us sound principles for life in His Word. Certainly we want to honor God in our words and actions, but thankfully

He doesn't give us exactly what we deserve. He shows us grace every day of our lives.

Aren't you glad that God doesn't fit into a neat little box? He is much bigger than our simplistic ideas. He is much broader than our mentality of, "If I do this, He will do that." He is a God of grace. Grace is unmerited favor, and as followers of Christ, we are recipients of God's unmerited favor. His blessed grace toward us means He loves us despite ourselves, and He has a plan for our lives despite our weaknesses and flaws. His grace extends beyond our sin, and He loves us with an abundant and unfailing love.

The Grace of Salvation

The biggest picture of God's grace comes in the form of His Son, Jesus. Jesus was God's gift to the world. The Bible is quite clear that none of us deserves heaven, because we are all sinners. Yes, to put it simply, "all have sinned; all fall short of God's glorious standard" (Romans 3:23).

Now you may be thinking, *But I've been a pretty good girl, and my good far outweighs my bad. God will surely let me into heaven.* If that is your thought process, we urge you to turn to the Bible to find out what God says about salvation. Not only does the Bible say that we are all sinners (with which we can all agree), but it says that "the wages of sin is death, but the free gift of God is eternal life through Christ Jesus our Lord" (Romans 6:23). We can't work our way, prove our way, or perform our way to heaven. Eternity with God is a free gift. It's amazing grace!

So if you are planning to perform your way into paradise, read the instruction manual again. It says, "For by grace you have been saved through faith and that not of yourselves; it is the gift of God, not of works, lest anyone should boast" (Ephesians 2:8–9 NKJV). Personally, we are so glad that we can't work our way to heaven, because the boasting in heaven would be painful. "Hey, how did you get here?" "Well, I served at a local charity, gave more than 10 percent to the church, and went to church three out of four Sundays every month." What a bragging match! We're so glad that's not how heaven will be.

Instead, it comes down to God's grace through faith. We don't need to *do* anything; we just need to *receive* God's free gift. Have you received the gift of His salvation through Jesus? Perhaps right now you want to open your heart and receive God's gift of salvation. You can pray to Him something like this: "Dear God, I trust You. I believe that Jesus came to this earth to die for my sins. I believe that He rose again, giving me promise of eternal life. I trust You for my salvation. Thank You for giving me the gift of eternal life."

You probably have heard of John 3:16 all of your life, but maybe you haven't taken it personally. Perhaps today is the day. "For God so loved the world that He gave His only begotten Son, that whoever believes in Him should not perish but have everlasting life" (NKJV). Notice that the verse doesn't say that "whoever *works hard enough*" will have eternal life. It says that "whoever *believes*" has eternal life. That's good news!

The Grace of God's Blessings

Perhaps you remember the scene from the movie *The Sound of Music*. In the gazebo late one evening, Maria and Captain von Trapp embrace one another after finally acknowledging their love. Maria then sings, "So somewhere in my youth or childhood, I must have done something good."[1] Such a lovely song, but not so lovely theology. God's blessings are a free gift to us. They are an overwhelming display of His grace toward us! Thank goodness He doesn't give us what we deserve.

David recognized God's gracious hand when he said:

> Praise the LORD, I tell myself,
>> and never forget the good things he does for me
> He forgives all my sins
>> and heals all my diseases.
> He ransoms me from death
>> and surrounds me with love and tender mercies.
> He fills my life with good things.
>> My youth is renewed like the eagle's!
> The LORD gives righteousness
>> and justice to all who are treated unfairly. . . .
> The LORD is merciful and gracious,
>> he is slow to get angry and full of unfailing love.
> He will not constantly accuse us,
>> nor remain angry forever.
> He has not punished us for all our sins,
>> nor does he deal with us as we deserve.
> For his unfailing love toward those who fear him
>> is as great as the height of the heavens above the earth.
> He has removed our rebellious acts
>> as far away from us as the east is from the west.
> The LORD is like a father to his children,
>> tender and compassionate to those who fear him.

For he understands how weak we are;

    he knows we are only dust. (Psalm 103:2–6; 8–14)

Truly God has given us more than we deserve. He has been gracious to us beyond measure. Now perhaps you are thinking, *If God's grace is so abundant, can't I get away with doing whatever I want and living however I please?* The apostle Paul was afraid we might say that! Listen to what Paul says: "Well then, should we keep on sinning so that God can show us more and more kindness and forgiveness [so that grace may abound]? Of course not! Since we have died to sin, how can we continue to live in it?" (Romans 6:1–2).

The truth is that God gives us kindness, love, forgiveness, and blessings of all kinds, which we do not deserve. Often we forget to recognize His gracious blessings to us, yet when we focus on the blessings in our lives, our attitudes become transformed. Stop reading right now and take a moment to reflect on all the blessings in your life. If you are going through a difficult time in your life right now, it may be hard to begin. You may find yourself struggling to think of any blessings in your life. We want to help you see that God has not left you, and His blessings are all around you.

Let's reflect on some blessings that are common to all who are reading this book.

- God loves you.

- God will not leave you.

- You are blessed with a precious child (or children).

- You have a job.

- God has created you with unique gifts and talents.

- God has provided salvation through His Son, Jesus.

- God has provided help to each one of us through His Holy Spirit.

Now that we have gotten you started, we want you to continue.

Thank You, Lord, for the blessing of the people in my life:

_____

_____

Thank You, Lord, for the provisions You have given my family:

_____

_____

_____

Thank You, Lord, for my church, for taking care of me in the midst of my challenges, and for the hope of the possibilities ahead:

_____

_____

The grace of God's blessings in our lives is manifold, yet we sometimes miss His grace because the negatives in our lives take all of our attention. Let's determine to continue to turn our faces toward the hope we have in Him and thank Him for His gracious blessings. We can take hold of the words of Paul: "Always be joyful. Keep on

> Grace
> so amazing and
> grace undeserved, I'll
> ever praise Him and joyfully
> serve. Grace so amazing
> and love so divine makes
> life worth living and brings
> joy sublime.
> —Gene Barlette

praying. No matter what happens, always be thankful, for this is God's will for you who belong to Christ Jesus" (1 Thessalonians 5:16–18). We may not be able to thank God for the bad circumstances in our lives, but we can be thankful within the bad circumstances of our lives.

As we recognize God's gracious blessings, we begin to see our attitude toward life change. We also begin to reflect His grace in our lives. Since we are recipients of such unmerited favor, how can we withhold grace toward other people? God's grace makes a difference in our hearts and in the way we deal with other people.

Glimmers of Grace

Sally had to live with her choices. A husband who was consistently dishonest. A life of uncertainty. An impending divorce. But Sally did not believe in divorce and certainly never expected her marriage to be counted as yet another sad statistic.

Sally's reality was tough. She had resigned from a fabulous job full of upward potential in order to accompany her husband as he finished the college degree she thought he already had. As he went to school, she began a catering business and gave tours of an elegant historic home—still hopeful that her life might one day be better. Unfortunately, things did not get better. Sally found herself in the midst of divorce, penniless and heartbroken. She was living in the reality of negative consequences as a result of bad choices.

When a life is shattered, grace glimmers like a sunset on th
vast ocean. It is like a lifeline thrown into the sea to one who
drowning. God's grace is the hope and blessed assurance that w
as believers can grasp as we reach up and seek God's guidanc
during the storm. Sally sought the glimmers as she worked tw
jobs and lived with a family member until she could get her fe
back on the ground. Slowly but surely, the glimmers of grac
turned to illuminate a pathway in her broken life. The pain wa
still evident but the sting was dulled. Why? Because she knew he
sins were forgiven, and she knew God's grace was sufficien
Grace means there is nothing we can do to make God love u
more, and there is nothing we can do to make God love us les
Sally used God's grace glimmers as steppingstones in putting he
world back together. Was it easy? No. Was it grace-filled? Yes.

As Sally began to anticipate God's grace gifts, she saw His loving
kindness blossom all around her. One particularly hard day sh
received a call from Donna, a college sorority acquaintance. Sal
had not seen or spoken to her friend since her college days. Donn
said, "Sally, I remember when you redecorated the sorority roon
and I want to hire you to decorate my house. When can we g
together?" Flabbergasted, Sally, not a decorator by trade, acceptec

Donna, a working mother of four, needed help; her time wa
limited and her responsibilities immense. While touring the go:
geous home, the former sorority sisters visited and shared idea
Sally began to get excited about the possibilities. As Sally pre
pared to leave, Donna handed her fifteen hundred dollars in cas
to cover the first part of her yet-to-be-discussed fee. Sally wa
astonished. She had absolutely nothing at this point; she ha
been searching for a job. But God gave her a glimmer of grac

that day just to keep her going. This gift so obviously had God's handprint on it, Sally was brought to tears. It was just the jump-start she needed as she strove to begin again..

Have you had glimmers of grace in your life? Take a moment to reflect on some of the significant ways you have felt God's hand on your life. We want to encourage you to write out your story and share it with your kids. As you do, you will find that your own spirits are lifted and both you and your children's faith will be strengthened.

Grace at Work

How does God's grace transfer to the workplace water cooler? Can grace be a factor in the nine-to-five grind? Does offering others grace make you a doormat awaiting the mud-soaked shoes of a coworker's advancement? Let's examine how to demonstrate grace in the day-to-day scenes at work.

Claire was in a predicament: a coworker named Ally often undermined her efforts. In fact, work was a scary place to be because Claire had no idea whom she could trust. She sought wise counsel and was advised to confront Ally in hopes of recti-fying the situation. She did. In the chilly corporate boardroom, the two got together with a third, nonbiased person present. Claire's heart was heavy; she knew things were not right, and her desire to change the climate within the workplace was strong. Claire spoke first, graciously listing her concerns and backing up her accusations with facts.

> God's grace is sufficient for us anywhere His providence places us.
> —Anonymous

Ally was shocked at Claire's kindness. In fact, the kindness took her so off guard that she admitted her competition and jealousy of Claire's abilities. Suddenly the walls of resentment, anger, and frustration crumbled. Miracles do still happen even in the workplace. Does this mean Claire's gracious attempt at reconciliation caused her work life to suddenly become perfect? No. It means that as light shone on the problem, it became easier to view the solution.

Grace at work doesn't mean you ignore or overlook a problem. It means you work through it graciously, reflecting God's grace and love. Here are some examples of grace demonstrated in the workplace:

- Showing kindness toward all, even those who don't seem to deserve it

- Speaking in love

- Holding people accountable for their actions when necessary

- Helping others become better in their work

- Doing your best without viciously competing

- Integrity and loyalty

- Demonstrating a forgiving spirit

- Practicing random acts of kindness

What situation at work needs a glimmer of grace?

_____

_____

What part can you play in rectifying the situation?

_____

_____

Grace at Home

Grace begins at home. God's grace is first extended from our heavenly home—a gift bought and paid for by Jesus. That same grace must be filtered down and shared in our homes with our loved ones. Why? If we cannot share grace with others, then we are placing ourselves in a higher position than God, who offers us His grace so freely. What does grace at home look like when you are exhausted and on your last nerve? What does grace look like on Monday morning when the kids won't cooperate and you have an early morning meeting?

Grace at home begins by recognizing our need for God's help and strength. Godly grace and love do not come naturally and are sometimes most difficult to display in our homes. So what do we do? We turn to our heavenly Father, who wants us to ask for His help. "Dear Lord, thank You for Your love and grace toward me. Help me reflect Your grace in my home with my family. Please give me the strength to be all that You want me to be in my home."

Let's describe what God's grace reflected in our lives may look like in our homes.

- Patience toward the slow ones

- Understanding and accepting different personalities and learning styles

- The law of kindness ruling our tongue

- Gently helping when your children just "don't get it"

- Disciplining in love

- Pragmatic, not dogmatic

- Flexible when necessary

- Discerning

- Tenderly teaching

- Listens with both ears to the heart of the issue

- Setting thoughtful rules and boundaries

- Showing mercy and forgiveness

Take a moment to ponder the situation on the home front. Are there areas that need a dose of God's grace? Do you need to consider stricter guidelines on certain issues, or is there an area on which you may need to adjust the rules? Are there rough spots that need attention? Take these issues before the Lord right now and ask for His wisdom, discernment, grace, and love. He will faithfully help you as you tend your precious flock, for He is the Good Shepherd who tends His sheep (see John 10:14–16).

> Grace is what all need, what none can merit and what God alone can give.
> —George Barlow

Grace Busters

In Dallas we have beautiful spring flowers and foliage. It's a true feast for the eyes! But the lovely plants are also a feast for little bugs. If we don't spray our plants with insecticide, there will be holes in all of the big lovely leaves. So we take all necessary precautions and preventative measures to enjoy the beauty that the spring flowers bring.

Grace is a beautiful thing that blossoms from our lives, but we must be cautious, for there are negative influences that tend to destroy its beauty. As we grow in our Christian character, we must become aware of the actions that eat away at the reflection of grace in our lives. Now don't get us wrong—nothing can steal away God's grace from us. Once we have trusted Jesus Christ as our Savior, our lives are "sealed for the day of redemption" (Ephesians 4:30 NIV).

What we are saying is that certain attitudes can nip away at the grace we ought to be extending to others and rob us of our joy in the process. We want to mention three grace busters that we need to guard against in our hearts: unforgiveness, bitterness, and anger. These three bugs hinder our ability to offer grace. Understanding these factors allows us to take action on making our home and work places of grace.

Unforgiveness

F. F. Bruce said, "The free grace of the Father's forgiving love is the pattern for his children in their forgiveness of one another."[2] Forgiveness is not easy, especially if you have been wounded by the wrongdoing of another. However, if we do not forgive, we carry a heavy burden that shows on our faces, in our stress levels, and in our homes. Typically the burden of unforgiveness hurts us more than it does the offender (who many times has moved on, unaware that we are hurting).

> True grace is operative and will not lie dormant.
> —John Trapp

By withholding forgiveness you are only hurting yourself. So if you need to forgive someone on your home front or in your business, get busy. How do you do it? The first step is to recognize that you are harboring unforgiveness toward another person. Then, recognizing that God has forgiven you of all your sins, decide that you will forgive the person. Forgiveness is an act of the will, not a feeling. Forgiveness is an act of releasing the right to hold something over another person. It is not a stamp of approval. In fact, if a behavior needs to be punished or changed, you may need to take steps to deal with that. Forgiveness is letting go of the grip you have on the injustice done to you.

Don't try to forgive alone; ask the Great Forgiver to walk alongside you and help you to forgive the person. The Bible says, "You must make allowance for each other's faults and forgive the person who offends you. Remember, the Lord forgave you, so you must forgive others" (Colossians 3:13). God tells us to forgive, and He will surely give us the power to do it. Once you have made the conscious decision to forgive, then you must also decide to change your thought pattern so that you will no longer keep thinking about it. In other words, release and move on in God's strength. As we extend forgiveness, we are freed to forgive and to better share God's grace with others.

Bitterness

Most people don't set out to be bitter people. Bitterness is not a quality most of us aspire to, but it seems to creep into our lives undetected and then grows into an ugly creature in our hearts. Where does bitterness begin? It can fester from unforgiveness, but it can also begin in the form of a thought or an assumption that we continue to mull over.

- She forgot my birthday, and I remembered hers.

- He got the promotion I wanted, and he didn't really deserve it.

- How could they discipline my child like that when I've donated so much money to the school?

- My parents were unfair to me as a child.

- No one helps me around the house. I have to do everything.

And the list goes on.

Bitterness may begin as a simple little thought, but if we allow it to roll around in our brains long enough, it simmers and brews and eventually explodes into full-blown cruelty in some form or fashion. What do we do with bitterness? With God's help we recognize and release it, much as we did with forgiveness. The Bible tells us to "get rid of all bitterness" (Ephesians 4:31). Again, if God's Word tells us to do it, He will give us the power to see us through it. Don't let bitterness fester and ruin your relationships or steal your joy.

Anger

The grace buster of anger comes in all forms and fashions. It can be a result of unforgiveness or bitterness, but it can also be a result of agitation due to our perfectionist nature or hurried lifestyle. If you find that anger is erupting all too often from your heart and spilling over onto the people whom you care about (or even perfect strangers, for that matter), then it is time to get to the heart of the matter and deal with it.

First, we want to ask God to help us see what we can't see about the anger. We need wisdom to detect the root cause. Try this anger-healing process.

Write down the top five situations or things that tend to ignite your anger.

1. _____

2. _____

3. _____

4. _____

5. _____

Now introspectively consider the root cause of these five things. What is it that deep down inside sets you on edge? Is it pride (you don't want to look less than successful), an overbusy sched-ule, bitterness or resentment, or a spirit of perfectionism? Write the root cause beside each of the five situations above.

Finally, think through a positive solution. What can be done differently? Do you need to forgive? Perhaps you need to take the picture of perfection off the wall and dump it in the trash. Write out your five solutions to the five problems here.

1. _____

2. _____

3. _____

4. _____

5. _____

Grace in Your Life

The first step toward moving away from the grace busters and moving toward a grace-filled life is recognizing our need for God and His grace in our lives. In His Sermon on the Mount, Jesus said, "God blesses those who realize their need for him, for the Kingdom of Heaven is given to them" (Matthew 5:3). Isn't it strange? Our neediness brings grace-filled victory in our lives.

Aren't you thankful that we have a God who loves us, blesses us, and offers us His help in living a life filled with grace toward other people? It is our hope that every one of us will choose to rid ourselves of unforgiveness, bitterness, and anger each day. We want to shine brightly as we reflect God's love in our work and home life. Because we have been given such a beautiful gift of grace from God, we can easily show grace to other people.

Without a doubt, God's grace makes a powerful difference in the way we view life and handle circumstances. As we grow in God's grace, we experience a very real and calming faith. Patsy Clairmont put it this way:

> A calmer faith. That's the quiet place within us where we don't get whiplash every time life tosses us a curve. Where we don't revolt when his plan and ours conflict. Where we relax (versus stew, sweat, and swear) in the midst of an answerless season. Where we accept (and expect) deserts in our spiritual journey as surely as we do joy. Where we are not intimidated or persuaded by other people's agendas but moved only by him. Where we weep in repentance, sleep in peace, live in fullness, and sing of victory.[3]

God's grace plays out in our lives in a practical way. As we continually place the circumstances and people in our lives in the hands of our loving and gracious God, we experience His peace. As we recognize God's grace toward us, we are able to demonstrate that kind of grace toward others. Most important, when our lives are touched by God's redeeming grace, we are forgiven, we are made new, and we are never the same.

> A man can no more take in a supply of grace for the future than he can eat enough for the next six months or take sufficient air into his lungs at one time to sustain life for a week. We must draw upon God's boundless store of grace from day to day as we need it.
> —D. L. Moody

What Is Your Spiritual IQ?

Which statement sounds most like you?

a. I am intrigued by historical evidence of biblical truth.

b. I find the universal search for God intriguing.

c. It is intriguing to see how nature itself points to the existence of God.

In which situation would you be most comfortable?

a. In a classroom setting where spiritual matters were explored.

b. In a small group of people discussing personal spiritual experiences.

c. Spending time alone in a search for biblical truth.

Which of these would you find most exciting?

a. Discovering an artifact that proved the truth of a biblical story.

b. Discovering that prayer is a two-way conversation with God.

c. Discovering that a relationship with God is attainable.

One of the great things God could do for me would be to

a. Provide answers to the things that don't make sense to me.

b. Bring fulfillment and purpose to my life.

c. Speak to me in ways I can hear and understand.

If I attend a worship service, I most appreciate

a. A sermon that helps me understand and apply spiritual concepts.

b. The experience of feeling somehow connected to something bigger than me.

c. The expressiveness and beauty of the music, singing, and prayer.

Spiritual truth is best taught through

    a. The presentation of facts and evidences.

    b. The lives of the ones who believe.

    c. Personal search and discovery.

Which of the following statements do you find most descriptive of God?

    a. He is omniscient (all-knowing).

    b. He is omnipresent (ever-present, everywhere).

    c. He is omnipotent (all-powerful).

Which concept do you find easiest to grasp?

    a. God has a plan for everyone.

    b. God will meet our every need.

    c. God is interested and involved in our lives.

My greatest spiritual need is

    a. To learn more.

    b. To grow more.

    c. To be more receptive.

Spiritual concepts

    a. Are difficult to understand.

    b. Are best learned through experience.

    c. Are learned by your heart, not your head.

Scoring:

If you answered *a* most often, *fact* is the basis for your spiritual pilgrimage. This means you seek to find answers upon which to base your spiritual response. Logic forms a major aspect of your search for truth. You dislike demonstrative worship services and emotional pleas. You have many questions about the why and how of things and are frustrated when the answers are not available. God gave us a mind, and logic is by no means antispiritual; however, some truths of our existence and God's nature must be accepted totally by faith. Finding answers is a valuable pursuit. The pursuit of God is a much more rewarding one.

If you answered *b* most often, *faith* is the foundation of your search for spiritual meaning. You have an innate awareness of your spiritual need. The search for purpose and spiritual fulfillment is inherent in your nature. Your instinctive inclination to the spiritual can cause you to be lured into unhealthy, cultish religions. Guard against spirituality for spirituality's sake. All roads do not lead to God. We are told in Scripture that the only way to God is through His Son, Jesus. Seek Jesus and you will find the spiritual purpose and fulfillment you sincerely seek.

If you answered *c* most often, *feeling* is the gauge you use in your spiritual journey. You have a very open heart and are sensitive to spiritual matters. You possess insight into profound concepts and are perceptive and discerning regarding the human condition. The very emotions that draw you toward the spiritual could cause hurt and disillusionment. Interaction with Almighty

God can definitely be accompanied by feelings and emotions, but you cannot base your spiritual life upon something as erratic and unpredictable as your emotional response. Spiritual truth is not based on our feelings. Our spiritual lives cannot be either. Truth is truth no matter how we feel about it.[4]

The Grace Factor at a Glance

- God's grace gives us relief and refreshment from our workaholic world.

- We must come to grips with the fact that God is not a performance-based God.

- The first step to dwelling in His grace is getting to know our glorious God, who so freely offers His grace.

- One of the most important things we can understand about God is that we can't understand God.

- Faith in God is freeing.

- Grace is unmerited favor.

- God's blessings are an overwhelming display of His grace toward us!

- Grace means there is nothing we can do to make God love us more, and there is nothing we can do to make God love us less.

meditations

for the frazzled soul

But he said to me, "My grace is sufficient for you, for my power is made perfect in weakness." Therefore I will boast all the more gladly about my weaknesses, so that Christ's power may rest on me.

2 Corinthians 12:9 NIV

For God so loved the world that He gave His only begotten Son, that whoever believes in Him should not perish but have everlasting life.

John 3:16 NKJV

Our high priest is able to understand our weaknesses. When he lived on earth, he was tempted in every way that we are, but he did not sin. Let us, then, feel very sure that we can come before God's throne where there is grace. There we can receive mercy and grace to help us when we need it.

Hebrews 4:15–16 NCV

You have been saved by grace through believing. You did not save yourselves; it was a gift from God. It was not the result of your own efforts, so you cannot brag about it.

Ephesians 2:8–9 NCV

And after you suffer for a short time, God, who gives all grace, will make everything right. He will make you strong and support you and keep you from falling. He called you to share in his glory in Christ, a glory that will continue forever.

1 Peter 5:10 NCV

Getting There

Simple Steps in a Positive Direction

Pay as little attention to discouragement as possible.
Plow ahead as a steamer does, rough or smooth, rain or shine.
To carry your cargo and make port is the point.

— WILLIAM ARTHUR WARD

Stanley, a veterinarian in Oklahoma, lived in a little town called Sasakwa. Everybody liked him, since he was a hardworking and wise vet. Because they didn't have enough people to hold all of the offices in the town, the townspeople decided they'd ask Stanley to run for sheriff. Sure enough, he was elected! Fortunately, he was a very good sheriff and a very good veterinarian.

One night quite late a telephone caller said to Stanley's wife, "Could we speak to your husband?"

The wife, trying to be proper, inquired, "In what capacity do you need my husband? Do you need him as a veterinarian or as a sheriff?"

There was a thoughtful pause and the caller responded, "Both. We can't get our dog's mouth open and there's a burglar's leg in it."[1]

There are times when two jobs are better than one! We should know. As both mothers (job one) and career women (job two), we can relate to the juggle Stanley felt with his two jobs. The trick is doing both jobs well and looking for ways that each one can benefit the other. It is our hope that *The Frazzled Factor* has helped set you on the path to doing just that!

In the weeks ahead, we hope you will reread the sections of this book you highlighted and underlined and meditate on the meaningful passages and quotes. This is not just a book to read; it is a book to soak in and apply to your life. We know that this book doesn't solve all of your challenges as a working mom, but we hope we have made your road a little less bumpy. Our hope is that through reading this book you will handle the pull of both motherhood and career with even more confidence and grace than you once did.

Becoming less frazzled doesn't happen overnight. It is a result of gradual changes you make, continually going in the direction you know God is calling you. As you continue to put into practice the principles you learned in this book, you will begin to see positive changes in both you and your family.

Our goal through this book is not to give you simplistic solutions to complicated problems. We do not want to simply pat you on the back and tell you, "Life will be great; everything will work out." But through the positive and practical tips you found in this book, you will be better equipped to make wise choices as a working mom. Choices and changes are what it all boils down to—making wise choices in the future and looking for areas that need to be changed. It's a day-by-day process.

Success doesn't happen overnight. Be gentle with yourself. Don't wallow in self-pity or regret for what is in the past. Move forward each day to be a new and better person, learning, growing, and being the light Christ created you to be in this world.

Know Thyself

In the book *Joy for a Woman's Soul*, Marilyn Meberg shares this personal reflection:

> We want and need to know who we are. Of course, for the believer, there need not be a puzzle. Specific attention, thought and planning about me took place before God actually formed me in the womb. That implies I am much more than a cozy encounter between my parents nine months before I was born. No matter the circumstances surrounding my conception, I am a planned event.
>
> Not only am I a planned event, I was "set apart." I have a specific task to do for God. We all have a specific task to do for God, and it was planned in his head before we were ever formed in the womb. That is an incredible truth!
>
> Not only is my identity and calling known, but also Isaiah 43:1 says, "I have called you by name; you are Mine!" (NASB). He considers me unique and set apart, and he calls me his own. May we sink into the cushion of joyful peace and never forget "whose we be."[2]

Aren't you thankful that there is a plan and a purpose for your life? As Marilyn so beautifully expressed, we are not a fly-by-night chance; we are a purposeful creation of God. Our job is to continue to seek our Creator and walk in His unique plan for our lives. It's easy to get bogged down in other people's expectations or in comparing our lives to someone else's. Let's run our own race and be the person God has created us to be.

As a former track coach, I (Karol) often told my runners to keep their eyes on the finish line. Never turn your head to look at the other runners; simply run the race that is in front of you. The only time we look at others is to help them, not to compare ourselves to them. My dad used to say to us as kids, "Compete, but don't compare." In life, as in running, we must run the purposeful race God has given us and not turn our head to compare with the other runners.

The woman described in Proverbs 31 is an example of a hardworking woman running the course set before her. She is a picture of a woman who fears God. She serves her God, her family, and her work. Although we can read this passage and sometimes grow weary in thinking of all she did, we must also remember that she is a description of all the wonderful qualities of a perfect woman, wife, and mother. Her flaws are not delineated for us, only her glories. Oh, if only our families saw our finer points and overlooked the negatives!

The Proverbs 31 woman lives with vitality. She embraces the tasks set before her with honor and responsibility. What task has God set before you? Are you willing to work heartily and cheerfully in honor to Him? Are you willing to give your family and work over to God, asking for His help and direction? Let's run our race well.

Humbly Walk in His Direction

Perhaps you recognize this poignant Aesop's fable. It speaks to the essence of knowing ourselves, being careful in that which we pride ourselves, and being grateful for the gifts God has given us.

A thirsty Stag came to a spring to drink. As he drank, he looked into the pool of water and saw himself. He was very proud of his horns when he saw how big they were and what branches they had. But he looked at his feet and took it hard that they should be so thin and weak.

Now, while he was thinking about these things, a Lion sprang out and began to chase him. The Stag turned and ran. As he was very fleet, he outran the Lion so long as they were on the open plain. But when they came to a wooded place, the Stag's horns became caught in the branches of the trees. He could not run, and the Lion caught up with him.

As the Lion fell upon him with his claws, the Stag cried out, "What a wretch am I! I was made safe by the very parts I scorned, and have come to my end by the parts I gloried in!"[3]

As mothers, we want to take an honest look at our lives. What are the positive aspects of our lives (blessings, gifts, talents)? What are the things that are working well in our lives? Are there some things we tend to scorn or despise? We also need to evaluate the areas in which we take glory or pride. Humbly we must take everything before the Father and see it in the right perspective.

Lord, thank You for the continual work You are doing in my life. Help me to recognize the blessings in my life and live in daily gratitude for them. Allow me to use the gifts You have given me for Your purpose. Guard my heart from taking pride in certain things (work, status, capabilities, etc.), and please do not allow these things to ensnare me or hinder me. Give me wisdom and discernment to live a life of honor for You.

We hope this book has served as an encouragement and support to you as a working mom. It may have also served as a sort of reflection pool to help you evaluate where you are and consider how you can best do what God has called you to do. He has a different road for each one of us. We can't compare our journey to another person's, but we keep our eyes on the Lord, looking to Him for strength and direction.

As we consider the essentials in life that are worth striving for, our list comes down to a very few. Henry Van Dyke summarized the essentials well in saying:

- To be glad of life, because it gives you the chance to love and to work and to play and to look up at the stars;

- To be satisfied with your possessions, but not contented with yourself until you have made the best of them;

- To despise nothing in the world except falsehood and meanness, and to fear nothing except cowardice;

- To be governed by your admirations rather than by your disgusts;

- To covet nothing that is your neighbor's except his kindness of heart and gentleness of manner;

- To think seldom of your enemies, often of your friends, and every day of Christ;

- And to spend as much time as you can, with body and with spirit, in God's out of doors—these are little guideposts on the footpath to peace.[4]

"Footpath to peace" sounds nice, doesn't it? Granted, our journeys may look more like a winding road than a straight path sometimes, but the little guideposts along the way are basic, and with God's help and guidance we will walk in His peace of mind and heart. Our prayer for each one of you as you journey down the road is that you will focus on the essentials and press on in the purpose that God has for you as a working mother. Most important, we pray that God will be honored in every aspect of your life both at home and in the workplace.

Proverbs 31:10–31

Who can find a wife of noble character?
For her value is far more than rubies.
The heart of her husband has confidence in her,
and he has no lack of gain.
She brings him good and not evil
all the days of her life.
She obtains wool and flax,
and she is pleased to work with her hands.
She is like the merchant ships;
she brings her food from afar.
She also gets up while it is still night,
and provides food for her household and a portion
to her female servants.
She considers a field and buys it;
from her own income she plants a vineyard.
She begins her work vigorously,
and she strengthens her arms.
She knows that her merchandise is good,
and her lamp does not go out in the night.
Her hands take hold of the distaff,
and her hands grasp the spindle.
She extends her hand to the poor,
and reaches out her hand to the needy.

She is not afraid of the snow for her household,
for all of her household are clothed with scarlet.
She makes for herself coverlets;
her clothing is fine linen and purple.
Her husband is well-known in the city gate
when he sits with the elders of the land.
She makes linen garments and sells them,
and supplies the merchants with sashes.
She is clothed with strength and honor,
and she can laugh at the time to come.
She opens her mouth with wisdom,
and loving instruction is on her tongue.
She watches over the ways of her household,
and does not eat the bread of idleness.
Her children rise up and call her blessed,
her husband also praises her:
"Many daughters have done valiantly,
but you surpass them all."
Charm is deceitful and beauty is fleeting,
but a woman who fears the Lord will be praised.
Give her credit for what she has accomplished,
and let her works praise her in the city gates. [NEV]

Notes

Chapter 1: The Guilt Factor

1. Harriet Lerner, *The Mother Dance* (New York: Perennial, 1999), 24.
2. Shari Thurer, PhD, *The Myths of Motherhood: How Culture Reinvents the Good Mother* (New York: Penguin, 1995), 91.
3. Laurie Whaley and Beverly Riggs, eds., *Becoming*, NCV Bible (Nashville: Thomas Nelson, 2004), 185.

Chapter 2: The Parent Factor

1. *God's Little Devotional Book* (Tulsa: Honor, 1995), 39.
2. Edgar Guest, "Sermons We See," *The Speaker's Treasury of 400 Quotable Poems* (Grand Rapids: Zondervan, 1963), 159.
3. Brenda Waggoner, *The Velveteen Woman* (Colorado Springs: Chariot Victor, 1999), 24.
4. Donna Partow, *No More Lone Ranger Moms* (Minneapolis: Bethany House, 1995), 13.
5. Elisa Morgan and Carol Kuykendall, *What Every Mom Needs* (Grand Rapids: Zondervan, 1999), 75.

Chapter 3: The Relationship Factor

1. Mr. and Ms. Wonderful Dolls are products of 2003 PNC, Inc. PM-31995. Made in China.
2. Alan Loy McGinnis, *The Friendship Factor* (Minneapolis: Augsburg, 1979), 21–22.
3. Jane Jarrell, *Secrets of a Mid-Life Mom* (Colorado Springs: NavPress, 2004), 123.

4. Glen Van Ekeren, ed., *Speaker's Sourcebook II* (Englewood Cliffs, N.J.: Prentice Hall, 1994), 317.

5. Dale Carnegie, *How to Win Friends and Influence People* (New York: Pocket Books, 1981), 54.

6. Vicki Iovine, *Girlfriends' Guide to Getting Your Groove Back* (New York: Perigree, 2001), 94.

7. Karol Ladd, *The Power of a Positive Wife* (West Monroe, La.: Howard, 2003), 192–93.

8. Laurie Whaley and Beverly Riggs, eds., *Becoming,* NCV Bible (Nashville: Thomas Nelson, 2004), 22.

Chapter 4: The Business Factor

1. Glenn Van Ekeren, ed., *Speaker's Sourcebook II* (Englewood Cliffs, N.J.: Prentice Hall, 1994), 175.

2. Jack Canfield, Mark Victor Hansen, and Les Hewitt, *The Power of Focus* (Deerfield Beach, Fla.: Health Communications, 2000), 101.

3. Henry Bosley Woolf, ed., *Webster's Dictionary* (Springfield, Mass.: G. & C. Merriam Company, 1974), 600.

4. Henry W. Longfellow, quoted on www.thinkexist.com.

5. Gwen Moran, quoted on www.BoostYourBiz.com.

6. Canfield et al., *Power of Focus*, 213.

7. Ibid., 48.

8. Kathleen Barton, *Connecting with Success: How to Build a Mentoring Network to Fast-Forward Your Career* (Palo Alto, Calif.: Davies-Black, 2001), 24.

9. Rick Warren, *The Purpose-Driven Life* (Grand Rapids: Zondervan, 2002), 275.

10. Roy B. Zuck, ed., *The Speaker's Quote Book* (Grand Rapids: Kregel, 1997), 128.

11. Dottie Gandy, *30 Days to a Happy Employee* (New York: Fireside, 2001), 25.

Chapter 5: The Fun Factor

1. *American Quotations* (New York: Gramercy, 1988), quoting from *Humor of a Country Lawyer* by Sam J. Ervin.

2. John Cook, comp., *The Book of Positive Quotations* (Minneapolis: Fairview, 1993), 7.

3. Charlie "Tremendous" Jones, *Quotes Are Tremendous* (Mechanicsburg, Penn.: Executive, 1995), 33.

4. Recipe for bubbles: 3 cups water, $\frac{1}{4}$ cup glycerin, $\frac{1}{2}$ cup dishwashing liquid.

5. Gwen Ellis and Sarah Hupp, eds., *Joy for a Woman's Soul* (Grand Rapids: Inspirio, 1998), 11.

6. Ibid., 15.

Chapter 6: The Rejuvenation Factor

1. "Power Naps May Prevent Burnout," *Nature Neuroscience,* July 2002.

2. "Stress Relief Through Exercise," www.Fitness-Equipment-Source.com.

3. Angela Beasley, comp., *Minutes from the Great Women's Coffee Club* (Nashville: Walnut Grove, 1997), 80.

Chapter 7: The Grace Factor

1. "Something Good," music by Richard Rodgers; lyrics by Oscar Hammerstein II; score for *The Sound of Music* (1965).

2. Jerry Bridges, *Transforming Grace: Living Confidently in God's Unfailing Love* (Colorado Springs: NavPress, 1991), 205.

3. Gwen Ellis and Sarah Hupp, eds., *Joy for a Woman's Soul* (Grand Rapids: Inspirio, 1998), 67.

4. Laurie Whaley and Beverly Riggs, eds., *Becoming*, NCV Bible (Nashville: Thomas Nelson, 2004), 133.

Conclusion

1. Roy B. Zuck, ed., *The Speaker's Quote Book* (Grand Rapids: Kregel, 1997), 416.

2. Gwen Ellis and Sarah Hupp, eds., *Joy for a Woman's Soul* (Grand Rapids: Inspirio, 1998), 48.

3. William J. Bennett, ed., *The Moral Compass* (New York: Simon & Schuster, 1996), 218.

4. John Cook, ed., *The Book of Positive Quotations* (Minneapolis: Fairview, 1993), 11.

About the Authors

Karol Ladd, formerly a teacher, is the author of fifteen books, including her CBA bestseller and Silver Angel Award-winning *The Power of a Positive Mom*, which has sold more than 130,000 copies. She is the founder and president of Positive Life Principles, Inc., and is also the co-founder of a character-building club called USA Sonshine Girls. Karol is a frequent guest on radio and television programs, sharing creative ideas for families and positive principles for life. She and her husband, Curt, have two daughters.

Jane Jarrell is the author of twelve books, including *Secrets of a Mid-Life Mom*, and co-author of twenty. A charter member of MOPS National Speakers Bureau, Jane is also a radio and television guest and has written columns for *HomeLife*, *Momsense*, *SHINE*, and *Heart at Home* magazines. Jane and her husband, Mark, have one daughter.